BEST EVER
family food

GW00359712

EDITORIAL
General Editor Jo Rogers
Editor Sheridan Carter
Food Editor Sheryle Eastwood
Assistant Food Editor Rachel Blackmore
Home Economist Anneka Mitchell
Food Consultant Frances Naldrett
Editorial Co-ordinator Margaret Kelly

PRINCIPAL CONTRIBUTORS
Catherine Saxelby Nutrition Consultant
Gabriel Gate Author Chef
Veronica Cuskelly Food Marketing Advisor

CONTRIBUTORS
Sue Amanatidis, Max Hosking, Di Johnston, Sue
Munro, Helen O'Connor, Jenny Ravens, Sue
Stuckey, Sue Thompson

PHOTOGRAPHY
Ashley Mackevicius

STYLING
Rosemary De Santis

ILLUSTRATIONS
Carol Dunn

DESIGN AND PRODUCTION
Karen Rickwood
Tracey Burt
Chris Hatcher

COVER DESIGN
Frank Pithers

DESIGN AND PRODUCTION MANAGER
Nadia Sbisa

PUBLISHER
Philippa Sandall

Published by J.B. Fairfax Press Pty Ltd
80-82 McLachlan Avenue
Rushcutters Bay 2011

© Australian Nutrition Foundation Inc/J.B.Fairfax
Press Pty Ltd, 1990
This book is copyright. Apart from any fair dealing
for the purpose of private study, research, criticism
or review, as permitted under the Copyright Act,
no part may be reproduced by any process without
the written permission of the publisher. Enquiries
should be made in writing to the publisher.

ISBN 1 86343 013 X

Formatted by J.B. Fairfax Press Pty Ltd
Output by Adtype, Sydney
Printed by Toppan Printing Co, Hong Kong

Distributed Internationally by
T.B.Clarke (Overseas) Pty Ltd
80 McLachlan Avenue
Rushcutters Bay NSW 2011
Ph: (02) 360 7566 Fax: (02) 360 7445

Distributed in U.K. by J.B. Fairfax Press Ltd
9 Trinity Centre, Park Farm Estate
Wellingborough, Northants
Ph: (0933) 402330 Fax: (0933) 402234

Distributed in Australia by
Newsagents Direct Distributors
150 Bourke Road, Alexandria NSW
Supermarket distribution
Storewide Magazine Distributors
150 Bourke Road, Alexandria NSW

CHECK-AND-GO

When planning a meal, use the easy
Check-and-Go boxes which appear
beside each ingredient. Simply check
on your pantry shelf and if the
ingredients are not there, tick the
boxes as a reminder to add those
items to your shopping list.

Contents

Introduction

Eating is one of life's great pleasures. Nutrition is vital to overall health and wellbeing.

The body is like a well-serviced car, feed it the right foods and it will usually run well. Try to run it on the wrong mix and it will be sluggish and not operate to peak performance. Lack of food can lead to poor growth and development, while too much food can lead to obesity and its associated problems.

We asked a number of well-known consultants and specialist dietitian/nutritionists to help put together a book that covers many aspects of nutrition. In this book you will find nutrition for growing up right, foods and recipes for sport, picnics and barbecues, delicious healthy desserts, parties for tots and teens, budgeting and spending your food dollars wisely, a guide to understanding food labels, nutritional analysis, and much more.

The Healthy Diet Pyramid plan is included for your quick reference when it comes to choosing nutritious food. From now on, choosing healthy meals and snacks will be so easy that even your children will want to be involved!

Healthy habits need to be nurtured in the home, encouraged in the school canteen and reinforced in the work place.

Good eating and better health!

Jo Rogers
National Chairperson of
the Australian Nutrition Foundation

NUTRITIONAL ANALYSIS EXPLAINED

Each recipe has been analysed for its content of kilojoules (calories), fat, cholesterol, dietary fibre and sodium (a measure of salt). At a glance, you can see whether a recipe is low, medium or high in each. This is useful for anyone watching their weight or on a special low-fat, low-salt, low-cholesterol or high-fibre diet.

Fat	Low – less than 20% energy from fat
	Medium – 20-35% energy from fat
	High – more than 35% energy from fat
Cholesterol	Low – less than 50 milligrams per serve
	Medium – 50-150 milligrams per serve
	High – more than 150 milligrams per serve
Fibre	Low – less than 2 grams per serve
	Medium – 2-6 grams per serve
	High – more than 6 grams per serve
Sodium	Low – less than 200 milligrams per serve
	Medium – 200-400 milligrams per serve
	High – more than 400 milligrams per serve

The Healthy Diet Pyramid

Good eating, good health

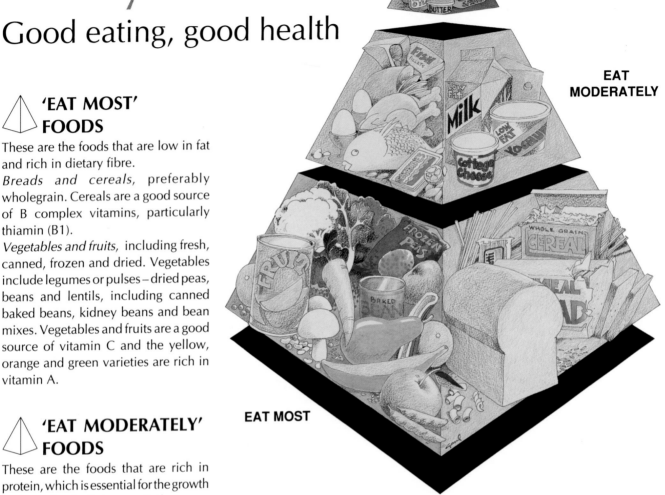

EAT IN SMALL AMOUNTS

EAT MODERATELY

EAT MOST

'EAT MOST' FOODS

These are the foods that are low in fat and rich in dietary fibre.

Breads and cereals, preferably wholegrain. Cereals are a good source of B complex vitamins, particularly thiamin (B1).

Vegetables and fruits, including fresh, canned, frozen and dried. Vegetables include legumes or pulses – dried peas, beans and lentils, including canned baked beans, kidney beans and bean mixes. Vegetables and fruits are a good source of vitamin C and the yellow, orange and green varieties are rich in vitamin A.

'EAT MODERATELY' FOODS

These are the foods that are rich in protein, which is essential for the growth and repair of all tissues. Both groups listed here are a good source of the B complex vitamins.

Lean meat, poultry (no skin), fish, eggs and nuts. Milk, cheese and yoghurt; use reduced-fat and low-fat varieties for adults and for children from school-age onwards.

It is safe to use some reduced- and low-fat dairy foods for young children once they are eating a mixed diet. But during the first two years children need regular whole milk to get sufficient kilojoules (calories) for growth.

If you want to reduce your blood cholesterol level, choose lean meat, remove the fat from chicken, prepare foods with little fat and use reduced- and low-fat dairy products.

EAT IN SMALL AMOUNTS

Margarine and reduced-fat spreads (including the polyunsaturated varieties), *butter, oil* (including the monounsaturates – olive, canola and peanut) and the polyunsaturated oils. *Sugar and sugar-based foods,* such as confectionery, jam and soft drinks. These are often the types of food shown on television. Children see soft drinks, confectionery and heavily sugared cereals advertised and want them.

It's hard to resist demands, but remember when it comes to overweight kids – prevention is better than cure.

DON'T SKIP MEALS

Skipping meals often leads to consuming more kilojoules (calories) not less. When you feel deprived, there's always the temptation to make up for it with a snack. For example, skipping breakfast makes a morning snack hard to resist. It has been found that breakfast skippers are more likely to 'break their fast' with sweet or fatty foods that are low in dietary fibre, such as potato crisps, pies, biscuits and sugar-sweetened soft drinks.

Missing meals also slows down your metabolism and makes it harder for your body to burn fat.

8 sure-fire ways to feed your family

Eating is one of life's great pleasures. Nutrition is vital to overall health and wellbeing. Put the two together and build a healthy and active life for your whole family.

1 **Feed your family** a variety of foods. Choose family fare from a wide range of foods. Let the Healthy Diet Pyramid be your guide. All the recipes and menus in this book are based on this plan.

2 **Watch that weight.** Not only can eating make you fat. It can make you ill. Being overweight or obese is one of the lifestyle problems of the decade. Rate the adults in your family by checking our Height and Weight Chart. If you are outside the range, then it's time to take stock. Turn to Weight Check (page 74) and find the answers.

3 **Cut back on fat.** Excess fat is a major problem because it is related to many serious illnesses. But we do need small amounts of fat in our diet, particularly monounsaturated and polyunsaturated fats, and that is why we use these oils and polyunsaturated margarine in our recipes. The fat-soluble vitamins A and D are found in butter, table margarine and reduced-fat spreads; vitamin E is found in vegetable oils, polyunsaturated margarines and reduced-fat spreads.

4 **Eat less sugar.** You can easily cut sugar from your diet. It provides 16 kilojoules per gram but no essential nutrients. Small amounts make the diet more palatable. So if you have a sweet tooth there is no need to avoid small amounts of sugar unless you are overweight. Sugar in a sticky chewy form clings to the teeth and sets the scene for tooth decay.

FIBRE FACTS

Fibre is nature's 'appetite suppressant' and bulking agent. It creates a feeling of fullness and may put a brake on overeating – important for dieters. It also helps with bowel regularity. Soluble fibre, found in oats, dried peas, beans, rice, barley and certain fruits, has the ability to remove cholesterol from the body. Unprocessed bran helps prevent constipation.

---

5 **Eat more breads, cereals, fruits and vegetables.** A healthy diet should include a range of fibre-rich foods, from vegetables, dried beans and peas, fruit, nuts, seeds to wholegrain cereals and wholemeal breads. Simply adding unprocessed wheat bran or oat bran to an otherwise ordinary diet does not bring all the benefits of fibre.

Carbohydrates are the body's preferred source of energy. Bread, potatoes, pasta and rice – excellent forms of complex carbohydrates – have often been maligned as 'fattening'. In fact, a slice of bread or a smallish potato has as few kilojoules as an apple!

DON'T PUT YOUR FAMILY AT RISK

Our great-grandparents were at risk of undernutrition and a lack of food. We are at risk of overconsumption of food and alcohol and too much fat, salt and sugar in our diet. As well as these excesses, our diet includes a lot of highly processed and refined foods, which lack dietary fibre. Today the major causes of illness and premature death in developed countries are linked with our lifestyle – the foods we eat, the drugs we use (including alcohol and tobacco), our physical inactivity and failure to cope with stress and get enough relaxation and sleep.

---

6 **Eat less salt.** A high salt intake puts you at risk of hypertension (high blood pressure). Cut down on salt gradually in cooking and at the table and you will not miss it after three to four weeks. More than 50 per cent of our salt intake comes from commercial foods, so it is important to look for salt-reduced and no-added-salt products when shopping. Do not salt food for babies or children.

7 **Limit alcohol consumption.** Many adults enjoy 'safe' levels of alcohol, but others misuse it and damage their health. Safe drinking for adults:
Women: Up to 1 or 2 standard drinks four to five times weekly.
Men: Up to 3 or 4 standard drinks four to five times weekly.

8 **Promote breast feeding.** Breast milk is the ideal food for babies. It contains the right balance of nutrients; it is easy to digest and absorb; it helps protect against infection and allergy; and it encourages a close relationship between mother and baby.

7 Day Menu Planner

Day 3

Breakfast
Orange juice
Untoasted muesli with low-fat milk
Wholemeal toast, spread with polyunsaturated margarine, reduced-fat spread or butter
Marmalade or honey
Tea, coffee or low-fat milk drink

Lunch
Wholemeal sandwiches - curried egg with chopped parsley and a little reduced-fat mayonnaise
Carrot and celery sticks
Low-fat yoghurt with diced fresh fruit

Dinner
Mustard Pork with Apple Sauce (p.12)
Mashed potato with low-fat milk and chopped chives
Peas with corn kernels and capsicum strips
Honey and lemon crepes (p.70)

Day 1

Breakfast
Orange quarters
Rolled oats with low-fat milk
Wholemeal toast, spread thinly with polyunsaturated margarine, low-fat spread or butter
Marmalade or honey
Tea, coffee or low-fat milk drink

Lunch
Wholemeal cottage cheese, grated carrot and chopped walnut sandwiches
Fresh fruit
Low-fat yoghurt or low-fat milk drink

Dinner
Lamb Cutlets with Plum Sauce (p.15)
Boiled jacket potatoes with low-fat yoghurt and chopped mint
Dry-fried sliced mushrooms
Broccoli or peas
Fruit Parfait (p.68)

Day 2

Breakfast
Melon wedge
Wholegrain breakfast cereal with low-fat milk
Wholemeal toast, spread thinly with polyunsaturated margarine, reduced-fat spread or butter
Marmalade or honey
Tea, coffee or low-fat milk drink

Lunch
Pita pocket bread sandwich (baked beans, reduced-salt; shredded lettuce and quartered cherry tomatoes)
Fresh fruit
Low-fat milk drink

Dinner
Stir-fry Apricot Chicken (p.12)
Steamed rice
Snow peas
Ice cream or low-fat milk ice confection
Strawberry sauce (p.68)

Day 4

Breakfast
Stewed Prunes
Toasted muffins with tomato and grilled reduced-fat, reduced-salt cheese
Tea, coffee or low-fat milk drink

Lunch
Vegetable Frittata (made with yolk-free egg mix for cholesterol-lowering diets (p.28) (hot for home lunch and cold for packed lunches)
Wholemeal bread, spread thinly with polyunsaturated margarine, reduced-fat spread or butter
Fresh fruit

Dinner
Tuna, Corn and Potato Bake (p.14)
Green beans or chopped spinach with pinch of nutmeg
Fruity Yoghurt Rice Cream (p.47)

Day 5

Breakfast
Mandarin quarters
Wholegrain breakfast cereal with low-fat milk
Wholegrain toast, spread thinly with polyunsaturated margarine, reduced-fat spread or butter
Tea, Coffee or low-fat milk drink

Lunch
Salmon Ricotta Dip (p.58)
Mixed-grain bread, polyunsaturated margarine, reduced-fat spread or butter
Fresh fruit

Dinner
Pork and Beans (p.44)
Winter Fruit Salad (p.68)

Left: Lamb Cutlets with Plum Sauce served with snow peas
Below: Stir-fry Apricot Chicken, Mustard Pork with Apple Sauce
Above right: Winter Fruit Salad

Day 6

Breakfast
Apricots canned in light syrup
Boiled egg
Wholemeal toast, spread thinly with polyunsaturated margarine, reduced-fat spread or butter
Marmalade or honey
Tea, coffee or low-fat milk drink

Lunch
Sliced Cheddar cheese, reduced-fat and reduced-salt
Pineapple Coleslaw (p.85)
Wholegrain crispbreads
Fresh fruit

Dinner
Family Roast (p.29)
(Beef with Red Currant Sauce, potatoes, pumpkin, baby squash and carrots)
Baked Apples with Prunes (p.65)
Low-fat milk ice confection

Day 7

Breakfast
Orange juice
Rolled oats with raisins and low-fat milk drink

Lunch
Pasta with Creamy Mushroom Sauce (p.16)
Mixed Green Salad
French bread sticks
Fresh fruit

Dinner
Fish Burgers (p.13)
Creamy Fresh Strawberry Yoghurt (p.68)

MENU PLANNING
Remember the Healthy Diet Pyramid
▲ Choose a variety of foods
▲ Choose more of the low- and medium-fat, cholesterol and salt dishes
▲ Keep the high-fat, cholesterol and salt dishes for occasional use
▲ Include some high-fibre foods each day

Growing Up Right

Children need the right foods to grow, develop and function well throughout the day. The old saying 'you are what you eat' is particularly true in the case of young children and teenagers.

Feed the body the right foods and it will usually run well, just like a well serviced car. Try to run it on the wrong mixture and it will be sluggish and not operate at peak performance. Insufficient food can lead to poor growth and development, while too much food, particularly foods with lots of fat and sugar, can lead to children becoming overweight.

Healthy habits need to be nurtured in the home, encouraged in the school canteen and reinforced in the work place.

WHAT'S IN FAST FOOD?

Fast food is generally high in fat, cholesterol and salt with little in the way of fibre – there are no filling vegetables, salads or fruit. Portion sizes are 'whopper' or 'super', making it easy to consume more kilojoules than you imagine. Because deep-frying is quick, convenient and appealing, especially on cold days, many takeaway foods are prepared this way. But it's a kilojoule-laden way to eat. The type of fat in fast foods is mainly saturated, the worst kind for your heart. Even if specified as 'vegetable oil', this can be one of the saturated variety, such as palm oil, which do not have the benefits of the unsaturated oils.
DO ORDER: Hamburgers with salad, steak sandwiches, Asian and oriental mixed dishes, pizza and barbecued chicken (with the skin removed).
GO EASY ON: Soft drinks, milk shakes, iced coffee, fatty French fries, potato scallops, battered and crumbed food, fried spring rolls, pies and pastries.

WHAT CHILDREN NEED

Follow our guidelines for planning family meals. Most days try to include:

Four or more serves of bread or cereal
One serve is:
1 slice bread
$1/2$ cup ready-to-eat breakfast cereal
$1/2$ cup cooked porridge, rice or pasta (spaghetti, macaroni or noodles)

Four or more serves of vegetables and fruit
One serve is:
1 piece of fresh fruit
100 g small fresh fruit such as grapes
$1/2$ cup canned or stewed fruit
$1/4$ cup dried fruit
1 medium potato or tomato
$1/2$ cup vegetables – salad, cooked fresh, frozen, dried or canned

One or two serves lean meat, fish or chicken, egg, nuts or legumes (dried peas, beans or lentils)
One serve is:
a medium serve of lean meat, fish or chicken without skin (about 100 g raw weight; use smaller serves for young children)
1 egg
30 g nuts or 1-2 tablespoons peanut butter
$1/4$-$1/2$ cup baked beans or any prepared dried beans, peas or lentils

600 mL milk
yoghurt can be substituted for milk substitute 30 g reduced-fat cheddar or hard cheese or 60 g cottage or ricotta cheese for 200 mL milk

One tablespoon table margarine
reduced-fat spread, butter or mono-unsaturated and polyunsaturated oil.

WHERE TO FIND IT

RICH SOURCES OF CALCIUM
Milk – all types, cheese, yoghurt, soy beverages with added calcium, canned fish, tahini and tofu

RICH SOURCES OF IRON
Lean red meat (particularly liver and kidneys), mussels, oysters, scallop and sardines, wholegrain cereals, cereals with added iron, wholemeal bread, dried peas, beans and lentils and green leafy vegetables

HEALTH AND CHILDREN
Many Australian children are already developing risk factors for the diseases their parents suffer from. A National Health and Fitness survey in 1985 showed:

▲ Half had levels of blood cholesterol above that recommended by the National Heart Foundation.
▲ One-third were overweight or obese.
▲ One-quarter of the 12-year-old boys had blood pressure levels above that recommended by the National Heart Foundation.
▲ 36 per cent of the energy (kilojoules or calories) in the children's diet came from fat (the recommended level for adults and children on a mixed diet is 30%).
▲ The average intake of dietary fibre for 12- to15-year-old girls was 15-16 g on the day of the survey .
▲ Girls 12 to 15 years, short on iron.
▲ Girls 10 to 15 years and boys 12 to 14 years, low on calcium and zinc.

In the Health and Fitness Survey, the sample was made up of 8484 children between the ages of 7 and 15 years. In the Dietary Survey, 5224 children between the ages of 10 and 15 years were selected from the same sample.

YOUR HEALTH
When parents and children share the responsibility for planning, shopping and preparing meals they are taking responsibility for their own health.

Different Ages and Stages

Children grow up so quickly, one minute they're babies and the next, teenagers. Each stage brings a new perspective.

Babies

Breast milk is the ideal food for babies in the first four to six months. If breast feeding is not possible, use one of the recommended infant formulae and follow the instructions of your health advisor or the directions on the can. Other foods are not necessary and should not be offered until the baby is four to six months. You should aim to have your baby on the family diet by his/her first birthday.

△ Progress slowly and let your baby decide how much.

△ Try baby cereal, finely mashed, or pureed potato.

△ Introduce new foods one at a time – try each new food for three or four days before adding another.

△ Do not add salt, yeast or meat extracts, sugar or honey.

Toddlers

Although food fads are fairly normal amongst toddlers, they do not last long and seldom affect long-term nutrition. Toddlers often seem to eat very little. Your toddler may do better with smaller meals and healthy snacks.

△ Check your toddler's growth in height and weight.

△ If your toddler is growing normally he/she is getting enough to eat.

△ Check fluid intake – keep milk to 600 mL and juice to 200 mL daily and offer water for extra fluid.

If toddlers do not want to eat family food:

△ Remember, they are learning to be independent and say 'no'.

△ Do not let them fill up on high-fat snack foods and biscuits, particularly just before a meal.

△ Do not make a fuss or force them to eat.

△ Healthy children will not starve; if you do not fuss they will quickly come around to eating.

△ Set a good example by having relaxed family meals.

School Children

Once children begin to eat some of their food away from home, they are influenced by other children and their teachers and what they see in shops.

△ Set a good example at home by preparing healthy lunches and including fruit and vegetables with meals on a regular basis.

△ Discuss food and fitness with them.

△ Encourage your children to be involved in planning meals, food shopping and preparation.

△ Discuss food promotion and advertising.

△ Take an interest in the foods sold in schools and encourage healthy choices.

Teenagers

The teens are a time of rapid growth and development. Usually appetites match needs, but some teenage girls are attracted to fad diets.

△ Teenagers express their newly found independence by giving up some of the family food habits and developing their own style.

△ Education and information about the best choices of snacks and takeaways are important at this time.

△ Remember it is the total diet that counts. Teenagers will eat some of the high-fat snacks and takeaways, but encourage them to balance these with foods from the Healthy Diet Pyramid.

△ Emphasise good food as part of a healthy lifestyle, which includes regular exercise and avoiding cigarettes and the abuse of other drugs.

△ Discuss alcohol. The most common cause of accidents and death in this age group is the abuse of alcohol.

△ Encourage teenagers to enjoy non-alcoholic drinks at their parties and gatherings.

What's for Dinner?

Try these delicious ideas for family fare. You'll find these simple favourites easy to prepare, satisfying yet light.

❖

SPAGHETTI BOLOGNESE

There are many versions of Spaghetti Bolognese but homemade is always the best. Add your own magic touch with a hint of garlic or your favourite herbs and create a special meal for the family. A crisp lettuce salad and crusty bread rolls complete the meal.

Serves 4

- ☐ **500 g (1 lb) fresh or 375 g (12 oz) dried wholemeal spaghetti**

MEAT SAUCE
- ☐ **2 teaspoons polyunsaturated oil**
- ☐ **1 large onion, chopped**
- ☐ **500 g (1 lb) topside steak, trimmed of all visible fat and minced**
- ☐ **425 g (14 oz) canned tomatoes, no-added-salt, drained and mashed**
- ☐ **3 tablespoons tomato paste, no-added-salt**
- ☐ **1 tablespoon finely chopped fresh basil**
- ☐ **1 tablespoon finely chopped fresh oregano or 1 teaspoon dried oregano**
- ☐ **2 teaspoons fresh thyme leaves or $1/2$ teaspoon dried thyme**
- ☐ **3 cups (750 mL/$1^1/4$ pts) water**

1 Cook spaghetti in boiling water following the packet instructions. Drain and keep warm.

2 To make sauce, heat oil in a large non-stick frypan and cook onion until golden. Add mince and cook, stirring for 10 minutes or until brown. Stir in tomatoes, tomato paste, basil, oregano, thyme and water.

3 Bring to the boil, reduce heat to very low and simmer, uncovered, for $1^1/2$-2 hours or until sauce is thick, stirring occasionally. To serve, spoon sauce over hot spaghetti.

2210 kilojoules (530 Calories) per serve

Fat	*13 g*	*medium*
Cholesterol	*65 mg*	*medium*
Fibre	*11.0 g*	*high*
Sodium	*70 mg*	*low*

❖

LAMB AND VEGETABLE KEBABS

Serve these colourful kebabs with corn on the cob and a crisp green salad. Cooked on the barbecue or under the grill they are sure to be popular.

Serves 4

- ☐ **500 g (1 lb) lean lamb cubes**
- ☐ **250 g (8 oz) cherry tomatoes**
- ☐ **250 g (8 oz) button mushrooms**
- ☐ **250 g (8 oz) zucchini, cut into pieces**

BASTE
- ☐ **3 tablespoons honey, warmed**
- ☐ **2 teaspoons salt-reduced soy sauce**
- ☐ **$1/2$ teaspoon ground ginger**

1 Thread lamb, tomatoes, mushrooms and zucchini alternately onto oiled bamboo skewers.

2 To make baste, combine honey, soy sauce and ginger. Brush over kebabs.

3 Grill or barbecue kebabs over a high heat for 8-10 minutes or until cooked to your liking, brush with baste and turn frequently during cooking. Serve immediately.

810 kilojoules (195 Calories) per serve

Fat	*5 g*	*medium*
Cholesterol	*80 mg*	*medium*
Fibre	*3.5 g*	*medium*
Sodium	*230 mg*	*medium*

NUTRITION TIP

With today's leaner cuts of meat you can enjoy a juicy steak, roast or chop, but remember to keep meat portions moderate. As a rule 500 g (1 lb) of meat will serve four people for dinner, as would four small chops or four chicken breasts. This is equivalent to about 125 g (4 oz) of meat or chicken per person — sufficient to supply all necessary iron, protein and B vitamins.

CHICKEN DRUMSTICK CASSEROLE

Removing the skin and any visible fat from chicken before cooking will result in a considerable reduction to the amount of fat in the complete dish. The skin is not difficult to remove, it pulls back easily and can then be cut off.

Serves 6

☐ 1 tablespoon polyunsaturated oil
☐ 12 chicken drumsticks, skin and visible fat removed
☐ 1 large onion, chopped
☐ 1 large carrot, sliced
☐ 2 sticks celery, sliced
☐ 1 tablespoon plain flour
☐ 1 small red capsicum, sliced
☐ 1 small yellow capsicum, sliced
☐ 1 green capsicum, sliced
☐ 1 tablespoon tomato paste, no-added-salt
☐ 1 tablespoon finely chopped fresh oregano or 1 teaspoon dried oregano
☐ 2 teaspoons fresh thyme leaves or $1/2$ teaspoon dried thyme
☐ 425 g (14 oz) canned tomatoes, no-added-salt, undrained
☐ 1 cup (250 mL/8 fl.oz) chicken stock
☐ 2 tablespoons finely chopped fresh parsley
☐ freshly ground black pepper

1   Heat oil in a flameproof casserole dish and cook drumsticks, a few at a time, until brown. Remove and drain on absorbent paper.
2   Add onion, carrot and celery to casserole dish and cook for 2 minutes. Stir in flour and remove from the heat.
3   Return chicken to the casserole, mix in red, yellow and green capsicums, tomato paste, oregano, thyme, tomatoes and stock. Cover and bake at 180°C (350°F) for 1 hour or until chicken is tender, stirring occasionally. Remove lid during the last 10 minutes of cooking. Stir in the parsley and season to taste with pepper.

860 kilojoules (205 Calories) per serve

Fat	10 g	high
Cholesterol	90 mg	medium
Fibre	2.6 g	medium
Sodium	155 mg	low

*Spaghetti Bolognese,
Lamb and Vegetable Kebabs,
Chicken Drumstick Casserole*

MUSTARD PORK WITH APPLE SAUCE

Serves 4

- ☐ 4 x 125 g (4 oz) butterfly pork steaks, trimmed of all visible fat
- ☐ 1 tablespoon wholegrain mustard

APPLE SAUCE
- ☐ 425 g (14 oz) canned unsweetened pie apple
- ☐ pinch ground cinnamon
- ☐ 1 tablespoon water

1   Spread one side of steaks with half the mustard. Grill steaks for 3-4 minutes, turn and spread with remaining mustard, cook for 3-4 minutes longer.

2   To make sauce, combine apple, cinnamon and water in a saucepan, bring to the boil, stirring occasionally. Serve immediately with grilled pork.

700 kilojoules (160 Calories) per serve

Fat	2 g	low
Cholesterol	70 mg	medium
Fibre	2.0 g	medium
Sodium	65 mg	low

STIR-FRY APRICOT CHICKEN

An adaptation of the ever popular apricot chicken casserole, this stir-fry is quick to prepare and is delicious served with brown rice and a green vegetable.

Serves 6

- ☐ 750 g (1¹/₂ lb) chicken thigh fillets, skin and fat removed, cut into thin strips
- ☐ 2 tablespoons plain flour
- ☐ 1 tablespoon polyunsaturated oil
- ☐ 1 large onion, sliced
- ☐ 1 tablespoon sultanas
- ☐ 1 teaspoon grated orange rind
- ☐ juice of 1 large orange
- ☐ 425 g (14 oz) canned apricot halves in natural juice, drained and liquid reserved
- ☐ freshly ground black pepper

1   Toss chicken strips in flour. Heat oil in a large frypan or wok and stir-fry chicken for 5-10 minutes. Add onion and cook for 2 minutes longer.

2   Add sultanas, orange rind, orange juice and reserved apricot liquid and cook for 5 minutes longer. Stir in apricots and heat through. Season to taste with pepper and serve immediately.

1000 kilojoules (240 Calories) per serve

Fat	9 g	medium
Cholesterol	85 mg	medium
Fibre	2.0 g	medium
Sodium	95 mg	low

> ### NUTRITION TIP
> Always buy lean meat from your butcher and trim off all visible fat before cooking. Remove skin from chicken and turkey.

Mustard Pork with Apple Sauce, Stir-fry Apricot Chicken

FISH BURGERS

A boneless fillet of fish in a burger is the perfect way to introduce your family to the delicate flavour and succulent texture of fish.

Serves 4

- ☐ 2 teaspoons polyunsaturated oil
- ☐ 4 x 90 g (3 oz) white fish fillets
- ☐ 4 wholemeal hamburger buns, cut in half
- ☐ 4 lettuce leaves, shredded
- ☐ 2 tomatoes, sliced
- ☐ 1 small Lebanese cucumber, sliced
- ☐ 1 tablespoon mayonnaise
- ☐ 2 tablespoons low-fat plain yoghurt
- ☐ 1 tablespoon finely chopped fresh chives
- ☐ freshly ground black pepper

1 Heat oil in a non-stick frypan and cook fish fillets for 2-3 minutes each side or until flesh flakes easily when tested with a fork. Set aside and keep warm.
2 Toast hamburger buns and top bottom half with lettuce, tomato and cucumber.
3 Combine mayonnaise, yoghurt and chives and place a spoonful on each burger. Top with fish and season to taste with pepper, cover with remaining bun. Serve immediately.

1530 kilojoules (365 Calories) per serve

Fat	9 g	medium
Cholesterol	55 mg	medium
Fibre	8.3 g	high
Sodium	935 mg	high

❖

SPLIT PEA AND FISH SOUP

Serves 6

- ☐ 1 tablespoon olive oil
- ☐ 1 onion, chopped
- ☐ 2 carrots, peeled and chopped
- ☐ 125 g (4 oz) cooked yellow split peas
- ☐ 90 g (3 oz) macaroni
- ☐ 425 g (14 oz) canned tomatoes, no-added-salt, drained and chopped
- ☐ 3 tablespoons tomato paste, no-added-salt
- ☐ 2 teaspoons chopped fresh basil
- ☐ 2 teaspoons chopped fresh oregano or 1/2 teaspoon dried oregano
- ☐ 4 cups (1 L/1 3/4 pt) vegetable stock, no-added-salt
- ☐ 500 g (1 lb) white fish fillets, cut into cubes
- ☐ freshly ground black pepper

1 Heat oil in a large saucepan and cook onion and carrots for 5 minutes or until onion softens. Add peas, macaroni, tomatoes, tomato paste, basil, oregano and stock. Bring to the boil and simmer for 15-20 minutes or until pasta is just tender.
2 Stir in fish and cook for 5 minutes longer or until fish flakes when tested with a fork. Season to taste with pepper.

1065 kilojoules (255 Calories) per serve

Fat	6 g	medium
Cholesterol	50 mg	medium
Fibre	4.4 g	medium
Sodium	130 mg	low

Fish Burgers, Split Pea and Fish Soup

VEGETABLE FRITTERS

These fritters are a delicious alternative to chips and a perfect accompaniment to grills and barbecues or as part of a vegetarian meal.

Serves 4

- ☐ **1 large carrot, grated**
- ☐ **1 potato, grated and squeezed to remove excess water**
- ☐ **2 zucchini, grated**
- ☐ **2 eggs, lightly beaten**
- ☐ **1 tablespoon self-raising flour**
- ☐ **1 tablespoon finely chopped fresh parsley**
- ☐ **1 tablespoon finely chopped fresh chives**
- ☐ **$1/4$ teaspoon ground nutmeg**
- ☐ **freshly ground black pepper**
- ☐ **2 teaspoons polyunsaturated oil**

1   Mix carrot, potato, zucchini, eggs, flour, parsley, chives, nutmeg and pepper in a bowl.

2   Heat 1 teaspoon oil in a non-stick frypan and add tablespoonfuls of mixture to pan. Flatten mixture slightly and cook for 4-5 minutes each side or until golden.

Drain on absorbent paper, set aside and keep warm. Heat remaining oil and repeat with remaining mixture.

390 kilojoules (95 Calories) per serve		
Fat	6 g	high
Cholesterol	110 mg	medium
Fibre	2.7 g	medium
Sodium	70 mg	low

TUNA, CORN AND POTATO BAKE

This recipe takes advantage of the convenience of canned foods. Prepare a salad or vegetable platter while it is cooking to serve as an accompaniment.

Serves 4

- ☐ **425 g (14 oz) canned tuna in water, no-added-salt, drained**
- ☐ **425 g (14 oz) canned whole new potatoes, drained and sliced**
- ☐ **425 g (14 oz) canned cream-style corn, no-added-salt**
- ☐ **2 tablespoons finely chopped fresh parsley**
- ☐ **freshly ground black pepper**
- ☐ **2 slices multigrain bread, crumbed**
- ☐ **$1/4$ cup (30 g/1 oz) grated fat-reduced cheddar cheese**

1   Layer tuna, potatoes, corn, parsley and pepper into a lightly greased deep ovenproof dish.

2   Combine breadcrumbs and cheese, sprinkle over tuna mixture and bake at 180°C (350°F) for 30 minutes.

1650 kilojoules (395 Calories) per serve		
Fat	13 g	medium
Cholesterol	50 mg	medium
Fibre	3.2 g	medium
Sodium	360 mg	medium

MICROWAVE IT

For an even quicker dish make this tasty bake in the microwave and prepare as described above. Remember to use a microwave-safe dish and cook on MEDIUM (70%) for 12 minutes. Serve immediately.

LAMB CUTLETS WITH PLUM SAUCE

Any jam – raspberry, blackcurrant or apricot – can be used in place of the plum in this recipe, just choose your favourite or what is in the cupboard. Cutlets are always a popular family meal. Corn on the cob, potato and peas make interesting accompaniments.

Serves 6

- ☐ **2 teaspoons polyunsaturated oil**
- ☐ **12 lamb cutlets, trimmed of all visible fat**

PLUM SAUCE·
- ☐ **2 tablespoons plum jam**
- ☐ **1 teaspoon prepared mustard**
- ☐ **2 tablespoons dry sherry**
- ☐ **2 teaspoons cornflour combined with $^1/_2$ cup (125 mL/4 fl.oz) water**

1   Heat oil in a large non-stick frypan and cook cutlets for 5-7 minutes on each side or until cooked to your liking.

2   Remove cutlets from pan and keep warm. Drain excess fat from pan.

3   To make sauce, place jam, mustard, sherry and cornflour mixture in frypan. Cook until sauce boils and thickens, stirring. Boil for 1 minute.

4   Arrange cutlets on serving plates and spoon over sauce. Serve immediately.

580 kilojoules (140 Calories) per serve
Fat	3 g	low
Cholesterol	40 mg	low
Fibre	negligible	
Sodium	45 mg	low

❖

VEAL GOULASH

Serves 4

- ☐ **500 g (1 lb) lean veal, trimmed of all visible fat and diced**
- ☐ **1$^1/_2$ teaspoons paprika**
- ☐ **2 tablespoons plain flour**
- ☐ **freshly ground black pepper**
- ☐ **2 teaspoons polyunsaturated oil**
- ☐ **2 onions, sliced**
- ☐ **1 clove garlic, crushed**
- ☐ **1 tablespoon tomato paste, no-added-salt**
- ☐ **3 tablespoons red wine**
- ☐ **$^1/_2$ cup (125 mL/4 fl.oz) beef stock**
- ☐ **3 tablespoons low-fat unflavoured yoghurt**

1   Place meat, paprika, flour and pepper in a freezer bag and shake to coat meat evenly with flour mixture. Shake off any excess flour mixture.

2   Heat oil in a large saucepan and cook onion and garlic for 4-5 minutes or until onion softens. Combine tomato paste, wine and stock. Add to onion mixture with meat. Bring to the boil, then reduce heat and simmer, covered, for 20-25 minutes or until meat is tender.

3   Remove pan from heat and stir in yoghurt.

860 kilojoules (205 Calories) per serve
Fat	5 g	medium
Cholesterol	105 mg	medium
Fibre	1.0 g	low
Sodium	210 mg	medium

Left: Tuna, Corn and Potato Bake, Vegetable Fritters
Below: Lamb Cutlets with Plum Sauce, Veal Goulash

TROPICAL SKEWERED HAM

Quick to prepare and cook, serve these tasty kebabs with minted boiled or steamed rice and a dollop of mustard. They make ideal barbecue fare and can be made in advance and refrigerated until required.

Serves 4

- ☐ **500 g (1 lb) lean ham steaks, reduced fat and salt, cut into pieces**
- ☐ **425 g (14 oz) canned unsweetened pineapple pieces, drained and juice reserved**
- ☐ **2 medium green capsicum, cut into cubes**
- ☐ **3 medium bananas, cut into pieces**

1 Thread ham, pineapple, capsicum and bananas alternately onto oiled bamboo skewers. Brush with reserved pineapple juice.
2 Grill for 8-10 minutes, turning and brushing with pineapple juice frequently during cooking. Serve immediately.

1110 kilojoules (265 Calories) per serve

Fat	*7 g*	*medium*
Cholesterol	*65 mg*	*medium*
Fibre	*4.0 g*	*medium*
Sodium	*1130 mg*	*high*

VEAL WITH TOMATO AND BASIL

Italian cuisine is always popular and this recipe is no exception.

Serves 6

- ☐ **1 tablespoon olive oil**
- ☐ **2 onions, sliced**
- ☐ **1 clove garlic, crushed**
- ☐ **6 x 125 g (4 oz) veal steaks, trimmed of all visible fat**
- ☐ **250 g (8 oz) button mushrooms, sliced**
- ☐ **425 g (14 oz) canned tomatoes, no-added-salt, undrained and mashed**
- ☐ **1 tablespoon tomato paste, no-added-salt**
- ☐ **1 tablespoon finely chopped fresh basil**
- ☐ **1 tablespoon finely chopped fresh chives**

1 Heat oil in a large heavy-based frypan and cook onion and garlic for 1 minute. Add veal and cook each steak for 2 minutes on each side.

2 Stir in mushrooms, tomatoes and tomato paste. Bring to the boil and simmer, uncovered, for 5 minutes.
3 Stir in basil and chives and serve immediately.

780 kilojoules (185 Calories) per serve

Fat	*5 g*	*medium*
Cholesterol	*100 mg*	*medium*
Fibre	*2.2 g*	*medium*
Sodium	*120 mg*	*low*

PASTA WITH CREAMY MUSHROOM SAUCE

This delicious pasta dish is certain to become a family favourite. We have used dried fettucine but if you wish 500 g (1 lb) fresh fettucine can be used in its place. The sauce is also good served with other pasta for a change – try it over macaroni, spaghetti or ravioli.

Serves 4

- ☐ **375 g (12 oz) dried fettucine**

SAUCE
- ☐ **2 tablespoons polyunsaturated margarine**
- ☐ **2 tablespoons plain flour**
- ☐ **2 cups (500 mL/16 fl.oz) low-fat milk**
- ☐ **250 g (8 oz) lean ham, reduced fat and salt, thinly sliced**
- ☐ **250 g (8 oz) mushroom caps, thinly sliced**
- ☐ **2 teaspoons finely chopped fresh chives**
- ☐ **1 tablespoon finely chopped fresh parsley**
- ☐ **freshly ground black pepper**

1 Cook fettucine in boiling water following the packet instructions. Drain and keep warm.
2 To make sauce, place margarine, flour and milk in a heavy-based saucepan over low heat. Bring to the boil, stirring constantly with a whisk. Reduce heat and cook for 2 minutes longer. Stir in the ham, mushrooms, chives and parsley and heat through. Season to taste with pepper. To serve, spoon sauce over hot pasta.

2260 kilojoules (540 Calories) per serve

Fat	*13 g*	*medium*
Cholesterol	*35 mg*	*low*
Fibre	*4.3 g*	*medium*
Sodium	*965 mg*	*high*

Tropical Skewered Ham, Pasta with Creamy Mushroom Sauce, Veal with Tomato and Basil

LAMB WITH MUSTARD SEED SAUCE

Serves 4

- ☐ **500 g (1 lb) lean lamb fillets, trimmed of all visible fat**
- ☐ **freshly ground black pepper**
- ☐ **2 teaspoons polyunsaturated margarine**

MUSTARD SAUCE
- ☐ **1^1/$_2$ cups (375 mL/12 fl.oz) beef stock**
- ☐ **1 teaspoon yellow mustard seeds**
- ☐ **^{1}/$_4$ teaspoon dried thyme**

1   Sprinkle fillets liberally with pepper. Melt butter in a heavy-based frypan. Cook fillets for 4-5 minutes, turning to brown all sides.

2   Transfer meat to a roasting pan and bake at 180°C (350°F) for 15-20 minutes or until cooked to your liking.

3   To make sauce, add stock to frypan and simmer gently for 5-8 minutes, or until reduced by half. Stir in mustard seeds and thyme and cook for 2-3 minutes longer.

4   Slice fillets diagonally and serve with mustard sauce.

720 kilojoules (170 Calories) per serve

Fat	7 g	medium
Cholesterol	85 mg	medium
Fibre	negligible	
Sodium	220 mg	medium

ABOUT PASTA

Commercially available pasta falls into three categories:

Packaged dry pasta which is available on every supermarket shelf. Cooking for this type of pasta is 10-15 minutes as it needs to re-hydrate as well as cook.

Fresh pasta is available from specialty pasta shops and is usually made on the premises. You will often see it displayed in bulk and it can be purchased in whatever quantity you require. The cooking time for this type of pasta is very short, 2-3 minutes.

Dried, pre-packed 'fresh pasta' falls between the other two and is available from supermarkets and delis. Cooking time is 3-5 minutes.

WHOLEMEAL PASTA WITH ASPARAGUS SAUCE

Serves 4

- ☐ **500 g (1 lb) wholemeal pasta**
- ☐ **2 tablespoons grated Parmesan cheese**

SAUCE
- ☐ **1 tablespoon olive oil**
- ☐ **1 onion, finely chopped**
- ☐ **1 clove garlic, crushed**
- ☐ **425 g (14 oz) canned tomatoes, no-added-salt, drained and chopped**
- ☐ **315 g (10 oz) canned asparagus cuts, drained**
- ☐ **1 tablespoon chopped fresh parsley**
- ☐ **1 tablespoon brown sugar**
- ☐ **2 tablespoons red wine**
- ☐ **freshly ground black pepper**

1 Cook pasta in boiling water following packet instructions. Drain and keep warm.
2 To make sauce, heat oil in a frypan and cook onion and garlic for 3-4 minutes. Stir in tomatoes, asparagus, parsley, sugar and wine and season to taste with pepper. Cover and simmer for 15-20 minutes. To serve, spoon sauce over hot pasta and sprinkle with Parmesan cheese.

2030 kilojoules (485 Calories) per serve

Fat	*6 g*	*low*
Cholesterol	*negligible*	
Fibre	*16.0 g*	*high*
Sodium	*190 mg*	*low*

❖

CHINESE BEEF WITH SNOW PEAS

Serves 4

- ☐ **1 tablespoon polyunsaturated oil**
- ☐ **1 onion, cut into eighths**
- ☐ **1 clove garlic, crushed**
- ☐ **1 teaspoon grated fresh ginger**
- ☐ **185 g (6 oz) snow peas, trimmed**
- ☐ **500 g (1 lb) lean rump steak, cut into thin strips**
- ☐ **1/2 red capsicum, sliced**
- ☐ **freshly ground black pepper**

SAUCE
- ☐ **3 tablespoons dry white wine**
- ☐ **1 tablespoon reduced-salt soy sauce**
- ☐ **2 teaspoons cornflour blended with 4 tablespoons beef stock**

1 Heat 2 teaspoons oil in a frypan or wok. Stir-fry onion, garlic and ginger for 2-3 minutes. Toss in snow peas and stir-fry for 2-3 minutes longer. Remove from pan and set aside.
2 Heat remaining oil in pan and stir-fry meat and capsicum until meat changes colour and is just cooked through.
3 To make sauce, combine wine, soy sauce and cornflour mixture. Pour over meat in pan and cook until sauce boils and thickens. Reduce heat and return vegetables to pan. Cook for 1-2 minutes to heat through. Season to taste with pepper and serve.

980 kilojoules (235 Calories) per serve

Fat	*9 g*	*medium*
Cholesterol	*85 mg*	*medium*
Fibre	*3.0 g*	*medium*
Sodium	*125 mg*	*low*

Wholemeal Pasta with Asparagus Sauce, Chinese Beef with Snow Peas

HIGH FIBRE MEATLOAF

Serves 4

- ☐ **500 g (1 lb) lean minced beef**
- ☐ **$^1/_2$ cup (45 g/1$^1/_2$ oz) rolled oats**
- ☐ **1 onion, grated**
- ☐ **1 medium zucchini, grated**
- ☐ **$^1/_2$ cup (90 g/3 oz) sultanas**
- ☐ **3 tablespoons evaporated skim milk**
- ☐ **1 egg, lightly beaten**
- ☐ **2 teaspoons grated lemon rind**
- ☐ **1 tablespoon lemon juice**
- ☐ **1 tablespoon finely chopped fresh parsley**
- ☐ **$^1/_2$ teaspoon dried mixed herbs**
- ☐ **freshly ground black pepper**

1   Combine mince, oats, onion, zucchini, sultanas, milk, egg, lemon rind, lemon juice, parsley, herbs and pepper.

2   Press mixture into a lightly greased ovenproof 25 x 10 cm (10 x 4 in) loaf pan and bake at 180°C (350°F) for 35-40 minutes. Drain off any liquid and stand for 5 minutes before serving.

1220 kilojoules (290 Calories) per serve

Fat	7 g	medium
Cholesterol	120 mg	medium
Fibre	3.4 g	medium
Sodium	145 mg	low

NUTRITION TIPS

▲ When stir-frying meat, cook over medium-high heat only until meat changes colour. Then add vegetables and liquid and complete the cooking. When using more than 500 g (1 lb) meat, cook in batches.

▲ Slice meat or poultry across the grain in approximately $^1/_2$ cm ($^1/_4$ in) strips. This ensures a more tender result when cooked.

▲ Avoid deep-frying and roasting in fat. Instead, grill, dry-roast, stir-fry, microwave, casserole or poach meat and chicken. If meat requires browning, brush pan with oil (don't pour it in) and cook quickly over high heat to seal in juices.

▲ Marinating is an excellent way to ensure tenderness and add new flavour to meat. And it has the added bonus of keeping lean meats juicy and tender. Try various combinations of aromatic spices and herbs with wine or low-salt soy sauce – garlic, ginger, bay leaves, lemon rind, mustard, chilli, rosemary and five spice powder are all excellent.

BEEF AND MUSHROOM PIE

Serves 6

- ☐ **4 tablespoons polyunsaturated oil**
- ☐ **1 onion, chopped**
- ☐ **125 g (4 oz) mushrooms, sliced**
- ☐ **425 g (14 oz) lean topside steak, trimmed of all visible fat and diced**
- ☐ **1$^1/_4$ cups (310 mL/10 fl.oz) beef stock**
- ☐ **freshly ground black pepper**
- ☐ **2 tablespoons cornflour blended with 4 tablespoons water**
- ☐ **12 sheets filo pastry**
- ☐ **1 tablespoon poppy seeds**

1   Heat 1 tablespoon oil in a large saucepan and cook onion and mushrooms for 2-3 minutes.

2   Add meat and stock to pan and season with pepper. Bring to the boil then reduce heat and simmer, covered, for 1$^1/_2$-2 hours or until meat is tender. Remove cover and return to the boil. Whisk in cornflour mixture, stirring until sauce thickens. Set aside to cool.

3   Layer pastry sheets on top of each other, brushing between layers with remaining oil. Place a 23 cm (9 in) pie dish upside down on pastry and cut a circle 2.5 cm (1 in) larger than dish through all the layers of pastry.

4   Line pie dish with eight cut pastry layers. Spread filling over pastry and top with remaining four pastry layers. Roll down edges of pastry and brush top with oil. Sprinkle with poppy seeds. Bake at 180°C (350°F) for 30 minutes or until golden brown.

1280 kilojoules (305 Calories) per serve

Fat	17 g	high
Cholesterol	35 mg	low
Fibre	1.5 g	low
Sodium	295 mg	medium

High Fibre Meatloaf, Beef and Mushroom Pie

19

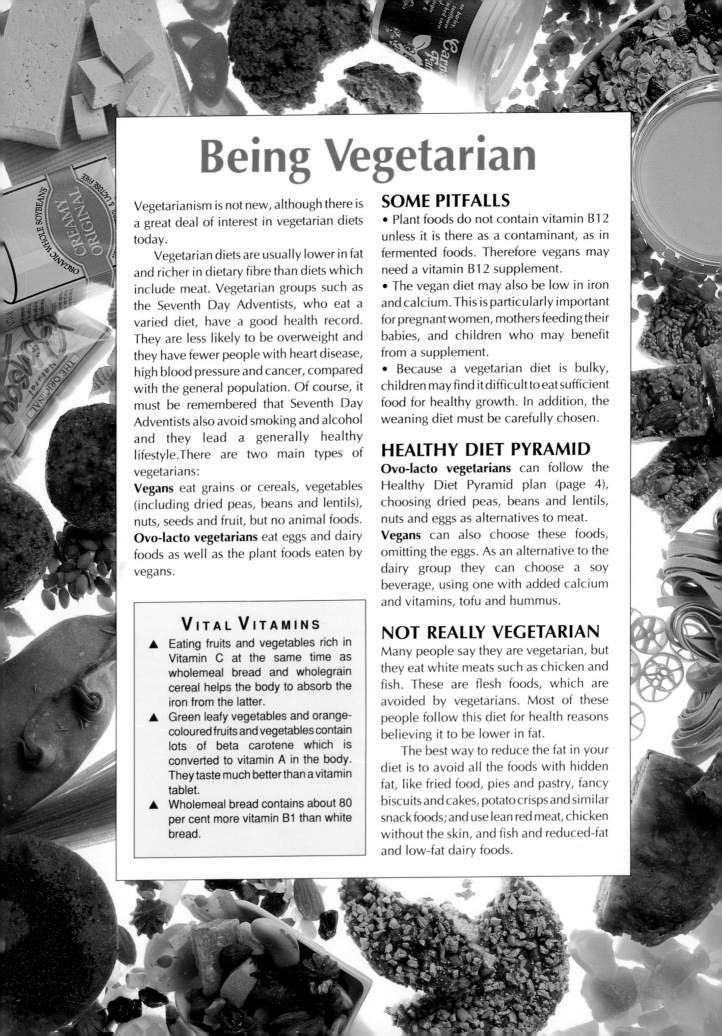

Being Vegetarian

Vegetarianism is not new, although there is a great deal of interest in vegetarian diets today.

Vegetarian diets are usually lower in fat and richer in dietary fibre than diets which include meat. Vegetarian groups such as the Seventh Day Adventists, who eat a varied diet, have a good health record. They are less likely to be overweight and they have fewer people with heart disease, high blood pressure and cancer, compared with the general population. Of course, it must be remembered that Seventh Day Adventists also avoid smoking and alcohol and they lead a generally healthy lifestyle. There are two main types of vegetarians:

Vegans eat grains or cereals, vegetables (including dried peas, beans and lentils), nuts, seeds and fruit, but no animal foods.
Ovo-lacto vegetarians eat eggs and dairy foods as well as the plant foods eaten by vegans.

VITAL VITAMINS

▲ Eating fruits and vegetables rich in Vitamin C at the same time as wholemeal bread and wholegrain cereal helps the body to absorb the iron from the latter.

▲ Green leafy vegetables and orange-coloured fruits and vegetables contain lots of beta carotene which is converted to vitamin A in the body. They taste much better than a vitamin tablet.

▲ Wholemeal bread contains about 80 per cent more vitamin B1 than white bread.

SOME PITFALLS

• Plant foods do not contain vitamin B12 unless it is there as a contaminant, as in fermented foods. Therefore vegans may need a vitamin B12 supplement.

• The vegan diet may also be low in iron and calcium. This is particularly important for pregnant women, mothers feeding their babies, and children who may benefit from a supplement.

• Because a vegetarian diet is bulky, children may find it difficult to eat sufficient food for healthy growth. In addition, the weaning diet must be carefully chosen.

HEALTHY DIET PYRAMID

Ovo-lacto vegetarians can follow the Healthy Diet Pyramid plan (page 4), choosing dried peas, beans and lentils, nuts and eggs as alternatives to meat.
Vegans can also choose these foods, omitting the eggs. As an alternative to the dairy group they can choose a soy beverage, using one with added calcium and vitamins, tofu and hummus.

NOT REALLY VEGETARIAN

Many people say they are vegetarian, but they eat white meats such as chicken and fish. These are flesh foods, which are avoided by vegetarians. Most of these people follow this diet for health reasons believing it to be lower in fat.

The best way to reduce the fat in your diet is to avoid all the foods with hidden fat, like fried food, pies and pastry, fancy biscuits and cakes, potato crisps and similar snack foods; and use lean red meat, chicken without the skin, and fish and reduced-fat and low-fat dairy foods.

CHICK PEA AND BASIL PATE

For the best flavour make this pate the day before it is to be served.

Serves 6

- ☐ **500 g (1 lb) cooked chick peas**
- ☐ **30 g (1 oz) fresh basil leaves, roughly chopped**
- ☐ **1 clove garlic, crushed**
- ☐ **1 small onion, finely chopped**
- ☐ **2 tablespoons lemon juice**
- ☐ **2 tablespoons olive oil**
- ☐ **60 mL (2 fl.oz) water**

Combine chick peas, basil, garlic, onion, lemon juice, oil and water in a food processor or blender and process until smooth. More water may be added if a thinner texture is desired. Chill well before serving.

770 kilojoules (185 Calories) per serve

Fat	9 g	high
Cholesterol	none	
Fibre	5.7 g	medium
Sodium	20 mg	low

SPICY SPLIT PEA RAGOUT

Ideal for a chilly winter's night, serve this delicious split pea and fresh vegetable ragout with brown rice and unflavoured yoghurt for a complete meal.

Serves 6

- ☐ **185 g (6 oz) split peas, washed**
- ☐ **3 cups (750 mL/24 fl.oz) water**
- ☐ **1 tablespoon oil**
- ☐ **2 cloves garlic, crushed**
- ☐ **1/2 teaspoon ground cumin**
- ☐ **1/2 teaspoon ground turmeric**
- ☐ **2 bay leaves**
- ☐ **1 large onion, cut into sixths**
- ☐ **3 potatoes, peeled and cut into 2 cm (3/4 in) cubes**
- ☐ **1 small cauliflower, cut into florets**
- ☐ **125 g (4 oz) green peas**

1 Place split peas and water in a saucepan and bring to the boil. Reduce heat, cover and simmer for 30 minutes or until peas are tender. Set aside but do not drain.

2 Heat oil in a frypan and cook garlic, cumin, turmeric and bay leaves for 1 minute. Stir in onion, potatoes, cauliflower and green peas.

3 Add split peas with their cooking liquid. Mix well and cook over low heat until vegetables are tender. If the mixture becomes too thick, add a little more water.

560 kilojoules (135 Calories) per serve

Fat	4 g	medium
Cholesterol	none	
Fibre	5.4 g	medium
Sodium	60 mg	low

NUTRITION TIP

Always use vegetables that are as fresh as possible. They should be well washed before cooking but not soaked. Remembering these two facts will ensure that you get the maximum nutritional value from your vegetables.

Chick Pea and Basil Pate,
Spicy Split Pea Ragout

CHEESY MUSHROOM TOMATO LAYER

Serves 6

- ☐ **2 teaspoons oil**
- ☐ **2 onions, chopped finely**
- ☐ **250 g (8 oz) mushrooms, sliced**
- ☐ **²/₃ cup (140 g/4¹/₂ oz) cooked brown rice**
- ☐ **125 g (4 oz) cottage cheese**
- ☐ **125 g (4 oz) cheddar cheese, grated**
- ☐ **1 teaspoon reduced-salt soy sauce**
- ☐ **2 eggs, beaten**
- ☐ **2 teaspoons chopped fresh parsley**
- ☐ **freshly ground black pepper**
- ☐ **2 tomatoes, sliced thinly**

1   Heat oil in a non-stick frypan and cook onions and mushrooms until tender.
2   Combine rice, cottage cheese, cheddar cheese, soy sauce, eggs and parsley in a bowl. Season to taste with pepper, add onions and mushrooms and mix well.
3   Place half the mixture in a greased and lined 25 x 10 cm (10 x 4 in) loaf pan. Arrange sliced tomatoes over top of mixture. Spoon in remaining mixture and press down firmly. Bake at 180°C (350°F) for 45 minutes. Cool in pan a few minutes before turning out.

1090 kilojoules (260 Calories) per serve

Fat	*13 g*	*high*
Cholesterol	*105 mg*	*medium*
Fibre	*2.4 g*	*medium*
Sodium	*250 mg*	*medium*

MINTED STUFFED ZUCCHINI

Serves 6

- ☐ **3 large zucchini**

FILLING
- ☐ **1 tablespoon olive oil**
- ☐ **1 small onion, finely chopped**
- ☐ **1 clove garlic, crushed**
- ☐ **¹/₄ teaspoon grated fresh ginger**
- ☐ **3 tablespoons slivered almonds**
- ☐ **155 g (5 oz) mushrooms, sliced**
- ☐ **1 tablespoon currants, softened in a little hot water**
- ☐ **185 g (6 oz) cooked brown rice**
- ☐ **1 teaspoon chopped fresh mint**
- ☐ **2 teaspoons reduced-salt soy sauce**
- ☐ **1 tablespoon lemon juice**
- ☐ **125 g (4 oz) tofu, mashed**
- ☐ **¹/₂ cup (125 mL/4 fl.oz) water**

1   Heat oil in a non-stick frypan and cook onion, garlic, ginger, almonds and mushrooms for 4-5 minutes or until onion softens.
2   Stir in currants, rice, mint, soy sauce, lemon juice, tofu and water. Reduce heat and simmer gently for 8-10 minutes.
3   Cut zucchini in half lengthways and scoop out the seeds, leaving a 1 cm (³/₄ in) shell. Pack filling into shells and place in a lightly greased shallow ovenproof dish. Bake at 180°C (350°F) for 20 minutes or until the zucchini is tender.

650 kilojoules (155 Calories) per serve

Fat	*8 g*	*high*
Cholesterol	*none*	
Fibre	*3.8 g*	*medium*
Sodium	*80 mg*	*low*

TASTY VEGETABLE AND LENTIL PIE

Serves 6

- ☐ **1 tablespoon oil**
- ☐ **2 onions, cut into wedges**
- ☐ **2 sticks celery, sliced**
- ☐ **2 carrots, halved lengthways and sliced**
- ☐ **¹/₂ small cauliflower, cut into florets**
- ☐ **2 teaspoons chopped fresh parsley**
- ☐ **1 teaspoon dried thyme**
- ☐ **750 g (24 oz) cooked brown lentils**
- ☐ **185 g (6 oz) walnuts, chopped coarsely**
- ☐ **1 cup (500 mL/16 fl.oz) water**
- ☐ **2¹/₂ teaspoons cornflour blended with 1 tablespoon water**
- ☐ **600 g (20 oz) mashed potato**
- ☐ **¹/₄ cup (60 mL/2 fl.oz) milk**

1   Heat the oil in a non-stick frypan and cook onions, celery, carrots, cauliflower, parsley and thyme for 4-5 minutes or until vegetables are tender crisp.
2   Stir in lentils, walnuts and water. Reduce heat and simmer for 5 minutes. Mix in cornflour mixture and cook for 2-3 minutes longer or until mixture thickens.
3   Spoon lentil mixture into an ovenproof dish. Combine mashed potato and milk, spread over lentil mixture and bake at 200°C (400°F) for 30 minutes.

1760 kilojoules (420 Calories) per serve

Fat	*21 g*	*high*
Cholesterol	*negligible*	
Fibre	*10.2 g*	*high*
Sodium	*75 mg*	*low*

FETTUCINE WITH EGGPLANT AND ZUCCHINI SAUCE

Serves 6

- ☐ **750 g (24 oz) fresh fettucine**
- ☐ **3 tablespoons grated Parmesan cheese**

SAUCE
- ☐ **1 tablespoon olive oil**
- ☐ **1 large onion, chopped**
- ☐ **2 eggplants, diced**
- ☐ **2 zucchini, sliced**
- ☐ **6 large tomatoes, peeled and diced**
- ☐ **1 tablespoon tahini (sesame seed paste)**
- ☐ **1 tablespoon honey**
- ☐ **1 tablespoon lemon juice**
- ☐ **1 teaspoon ground turmeric**
- ☐ **pinch cayenne pepper**

1   Cook fettucine in boiling water for 3-5 minutes. Drain and keep warm.
2   To make sauce, heat oil in frypan and cook onion for 2-3 minutes or until golden. Stir in the eggplant, zucchini and tomatoes, cook for 2-3 minutes longer. Add tahini, honey, lemon juice, turmeric and pepper, reduce heat, cover and simmer for 30 minutes. To serve, spoon sauce over hot fettucine and sprinkle with Parmesan cheese.

1910 kilojoules (455 Calories) per serve

Fat	*7 g*	*low*
Cholesterol	*negligible*	
Fibre	*9.1 g*	*high*
Sodium	*50 mg*	*low*

NUTRITION TIP

A platter of crisp raw vegetables is a good way to start off a dinner party. Guests can nibble on them or dunk into a yoghurt dip in place of cracker biscuits. They are light and refreshing and won't spoil your appetite for the main course. An easy yoghurt dip can be made by combining 1 cup (250 g/8 oz) low-fat unflavoured yoghurt, 1 teaspoon lemon juice and finely chopped fresh herbs.

Tasty Vegetable and Lentil Pie,
Cheesy Mushroom Tomato Layer,
Minted Stuffed Zucchini

VEGETABLE	STEAM	BOIL Note: Bring water to the boil before adding vegetables	MICROWAVE Note: Cook vegetables on HIGH (100%) and always cover before microwaving
Asparagus	15 mins	8-10	500 g (1 lb) 5-6 mins
Beans – Green, Runner	15 mins	8-10	500 g (1 lb) 8 mins and $^1/_2$ cup (125 mL) water
Beans – Broad	20-30 mins	15-20 mins	500 g (1 lb) 8-10 mins and $^1/_4$ cup (60 mL) water
Beetroot		30-40 mins	500 g (1 lb) 15 mins
Broccoli	10-15 mins	5-10 mins	500 g (1 lb) 5 mins
Brussels Sprouts	15-10 mins	10 mins	500 g (1 lb) 5-6 mins
Cabbage	5-10 mins	3-5 mins	500 g (1 lb) 4-5 mins
Carrots	20-25 mins	15-20 mins	500 g (1 lb) 8-10 mins
Cauliflower	10-15 mins	8-10 mins	500 g (1 lb) 6-8 mins
Celery	10-15 mins	5 mins	500 g (1 lb) 4-5 mins
Eggplant			500 g (1 lb) 5-8 mins
Leeks	15-20 mins	10-15 mins	500 g (1 lb) 5-6 mins

VEGETABLE	STEAM	BOIL Note: Bring water to the boil before adding vegetables	MICROWAVE Note: Cook vegetables on HIGH (100%) and always cover before microwaving
Marrow		10-15 mins	500 g (1 lb) 5 mins
Mushrooms			500 g (1 lb) 4-5 mins
Onions	20-30 mins	20-30 mins	500 g (1 lb) 6-8 mins
Parsnips	20-25 mins	15-20 mins	500 g (1 lb) 8-10 mins
Peas	15-20 mins	10-15 mins	500g (1 lb) 4-5 mins
Potatoes – New	25-30 mins	15-25 mins	500 g (1 lb) 8-10 mins
Potatoes – Old	30-45 mins	25-40 mins	500 g (1 lb) 10-12 mins
Pumpkin	35-45 mins	20-30 mins	500 g (1 lb) 10 mins
Silverbeet	10-15 mins	5-10 mins	500 g (1 lb) 4-5 mins
Snow Peas	5-8 mins	3-5 mins	500 g (1 lb) 3-4 mins
Spinach	10-15 mins	5-10 mins	500 g (1 lb) 4-5 mins
Zucchini/Courgette	5-10 mins	5-10 mins	500 g (1 lb) 4-5 mins

Something Light

Light, fresh food – whether it is a crisp salad or a vegetable frittata – is delicious, easy and a pleasure to prepare.

❖ WARM SEAFOOD SALAD

Serves 6

- ☐ 1 mignonette lettuce, torn into even pieces
- ☐ 12 large mint leaves, finely sliced
- ☐ 280 g (9 oz) cooked fresh asparagus or 350 g (11 oz) canned asparagus, no-added-salt, drained
- ☐ 1 tablespoon olive oil
- ☐ 250 g (8 oz) white fish fillets, cut into thin strips
- ☐ 250 g (8 oz) fresh scallops, trimmed
- ☐ 250 g (8 oz) green prawns, peeled and deveined
- ☐ 2 tablespoons lemon or lime juice

1 Arrange lettuce, mint and asparagus on a large serving platter or six individual serving plates.
2 Heat oil in a large non-stick frypan or on a cast iron grill and cook fish, scallops and prawns for 3 minutes. Add lemon juice and cook for 1 minute longer. Top salad with seafood and serve immediately.

700 kilojoules (170 Calories) per serve

Fat	*6 g*	*medium*
Cholesterol	*125 mg*	*medium*
Fibre	*1.1 g*	*low*
Sodium	*245 mg*	*medium*

❖ HOT COLESLAW

Served with baked potatoes or crusty bread this unusual coleslaw makes a light yet filling meal.

Serves 4

- ☐ 1 bacon rasher, chopped
- ☐ 1/2 cabbage, shredded
- ☐ 2 green apples, coarsely chopped
- ☐ 1/2 teaspoon nutmeg

DRESSING
- ☐ 1 clove garlic, crushed
- ☐ 2 tablespoon cider vinegar
- ☐ 1 teaspoon sesame oil
- ☐ 2 teaspoons polyunsaturated oil
- ☐ freshly ground black pepper

1 Cook bacon in a non-stick frypan until just crisp. Add cabbage and apples and toss well. Cook for 3-4 minutes then mix in nutmeg. Using a slotted spoon, transfer to a warmed bowl and toss to combine.
2 To make dressing, combine garlic, vinegar, oils, and pepper to taste, in a screwtop jar and shake well. Pour over coleslaw and serve.

480 kilojoules (115 Calories) per serve

Fat	*7 g*	*high*
Cholesterol	*6 mg*	*low*
Fibre	*4.6 g*	*medium*
Sodium	*200 mg*	*medium*

❖ BEEF AND BEAN SOUP

A filling soup which makes a wonderful winter meal. Serve accompanied by crusty grain rolls, garlic or herb bread.

Serves 4

- ☐ 2 teaspoons polyunsaturated oil
- ☐ 1 large onion, chopped
- ☐ 375 g (12 oz) topside steak, trimmed of all visible fat and minced
- ☐ 250 g (8 oz) pumpkin, cut into cubes
- ☐ 2 sticks celery, diced
- ☐ 3 cups (750 mL/1 1/4 pt) beef stock
- ☐ 425 g (14 oz) canned three bean mix, drained
- ☐ freshly ground black pepper
- ☐ 2 tablespoons finely chopped fresh parsley

1 Heat oil in a large saucepan and cook onion and steak for 5 minutes or until brown.
2 Stir in pumpkin, celery and stock. Cover, bring to the boil and simmer for 1 hour. Add bean mix and bring to the boil. Season to taste with pepper and stir in parsley.

960 kilojoules (230 Calories) per serve

Fat	*7 g*	*medium*
Cholesterol	*55 mg*	*medium*
Fibre	*7.6 g*	*high*
Sodium	*665 mg*	*high*

PEANUT LAMB POCKETS

An interesting way to use leftover roast lamb, these tasty pockets are sure to become a family favourite. Any vegetables may be used according to your family's taste.

Serves 4

- ☐ 6 small wholemeal pita breads, cut in half
- ☐ 375 g (12 oz) cooked lean lamb strips or leftover lamb roast, sliced
- ☐ 30 g (1 oz) bean sprouts
- ☐ 1 large carrot, grated
- ☐ 125 g (4 oz) beans, sliced

PEANUT SAUCE
- ☐ 3 tablespoons crunchy unsalted peanut butter
- ☐ 1 clove garlic, crushed
- ☐ pinch chilli powder
- ☐ 90 g (3 oz) low-fat unflavoured yoghurt

1 To make sauce, place peanut butter, garlic, chilli powder and yoghurt in food processor or blender and process until smooth.
2 Spread inside of pita breads with sauce and fill with lamb, bean sprouts, carrot and beans.

2470 kilojoules (590 Calories) per serve
Fat	*21 g*	*medium*
Cholesterol	*105 mg*	*medium*
Fibre	*10.4 g*	*high*
Sodium	*985 mg*	*high*

NUTRITION TIP

▲ Combine small to medium serves of meat with lots of potato, pasta, rice or even a bean salad, all popular as well as nutritious. When serving meat, remember that lean meat is more appetising than fatty meat.

▲ Measure salad dressings carefully so as to use only what is needed – salad dressings are rich in fat and kilojoules.

Warm Seafood Salad,
Beef and Bean Soup,
Peanut Lamb Pockets

CITRUS CHICKEN SALAD

A great dish for picnics or outdoor eating.

Serves 4

- ☐ 375 g (12 oz) cooked skinless chicken fillets, cut into strips
- ☐ 1 cup (250 g/8 oz) cooked vegeroni noodles, drained, rinsed and cooled
- ☐ 4 shallots, diced
- ☐ 1 orange, cut into pieces
- ☐ juice of 1 orange
- ☐ 1 teaspoon salt-reduced soy sauce
- ☐ freshly ground black pepper

1   Place chicken, noodles, shallots and orange pieces in a salad bowl. Toss to combine.

2   Combine orange juice and soy sauce. Pour over salad and toss to coat ingredients. Season to taste with pepper. Refrigerate until ready to serve.

900 kilojoules (215 Calories) per serve

Fat	5 g	low
Cholesterol	85 mg	medium
Fibre	1.5 g	low
Sodium	135 mg	low

VEGETABLE FRITTATA

Frittata is the Italian farmer's version of a French omelette. It is quick and easy to prepare and a great way of using up odd vegetables. Serve with a crisp salad for a light meal.

Serves 4

- ☐ 1 tablespoon polyunsaturated margarine
- ☐ 1 large onion, diced
- ☐ 2 zucchini, sliced
- ☐ 2 large tomatoes, chopped
- ☐ 3 flat mushrooms, sliced
- ☐ 125 g (4 oz) canned corn kernels, no-added-salt, drained
- ☐ 4 eggs, lightly beaten
- ☐ 1 tablespoon finely chopped fresh basil
- ☐ 1 tablespoon finely chopped fresh mint
- ☐ 1 tablespoon grated Parmesan cheese
- ☐ freshly ground black pepper

1   Heat margarine in a non-stick frypan and cook onion, zucchini, tomatoes and mushrooms for 5 minutes or until vegetables are just tender.

2   Stir in corn, eggs, basil, mint, and Parmesan cheese. Season to taste with pepper. Cook over a low heat until just set. Cut into wedges and serve immediately.

760 kilojoules (180 Calories) per serve

Fat	11 g	high
Cholesterol	225 mg	medium
Fibre	5.5 g	medium
Sodium	100 mg	low

NUTRITION TIP

When using meat juices from a roast to make gravy, add a handful of ice cubes to the gravy pan before starting. You will quickly see the fat become solid, and easy to remove – you are left with clear meat juice for a most flavoursome gravy.

Below: Citrus Chicken Salad, Vegetable Frittata
Right: Family Roast

LIGHT AND EASY

❖

FAMILY ROAST

There is nothing quite like a roast. It is the meal everyone looks forward to and is ideal for special family occasions.

Serves 4

- ☐ **1 lean corner piece topside or silverside, trimmed of all visible fat**
- ☐ **1 tablespoon polyunsaturated vegetable oil**
- ☐ **4 medium potatoes, halved**
- ☐ **250 g (8 oz) pumpkin, cut into chunks**
- ☐ **500 g (16 oz) baby squash or zucchini**

SEASONING
- ☐ **3 slices multigrain bread, crusts removed and crumbed**
- ☐ **2 tablespoons finely chopped fresh parsley**
- ☐ **1 teaspoon finely chopped fresh sage or $^1/_4$ teaspoon dried sage**
- ☐ **1 small onion, finely chopped**
- ☐ **1 teaspoon fresh thyme leaves or $^1/_4$ teaspoon dried thyme**
- ☐ **$^1/_4$ teaspoon white pepper**
- ☐ **1 egg, lightly beaten**

REDCURRANT SAUCE
- ☐ **2 tablespoons cornflour**
- ☐ **2 cups (500 mL/16 fl.oz) beef stock**
- ☐ **1 tablespoon redcurrant jelly**

1 To make seasoning, combine breadcrumbs, parsley, sage, onion, thyme and pepper in a bowl. Add egg and mix well.

2 Cut a pocket in side of beef by inserting a knife and cutting almost to the back and sides. Place seasoning in pocket and secure with skewers. Weigh beef to calculate cooking time.

3 Place beef on a roasting rack, over a baking dish, with water covering the base. Roast beef, allowing 20-25 minutes per 500 g (1 lb) for rare, 25-30 minutes for medium and 30-35 minutes for well done.

Remove, cover and set aside for 10-15 minutes before carving.

4 Place oil, potatoes and pumpkin in a separate roasting dish and place in oven with beef for the last hour of cooking. After beef is removed from oven, increase temperature to 220°C (425°F) and cook vegetables for 5-10 minutes longer or until crisp.

5 Steam or microwave squash for 5-6 minutes or until just tender.

6 To make sauce, skim any fat from roasting pan. Blend cornflour and stock and add to pan juices. Bring to the boil, stirring until thickened. Stir in the redcurrant jelly. Serve beef sliced with vegetables and sauce.

1820 kilojoules (435 Calories) per serve

Fat	*19 g*	*high*
Cholesterol	*125 mg*	*medium*
Fibre	*8.2 g*	*high*
Sodium	*375 mg*	*medium*

Easy Ways to Cut Fat

It makes good sense to cut back on the fat you eat for the sake of your health, and your waistline.

A small amount of fat is required for health and growth, but the average intake is far in excess of this. Around 36 per cent of the kilojoules (calories) we eat is in the form of fat. This should be reduced to 30 per cent or less. Fat has twice as many kilojoules (calories) as protein or carbohydrates, when compared on a weight-for-weight basis.

FAT IN OUR FOODS

Most of the fat in the average diet is derived from meat, poultry and meat products (such as bacon, ham, sausage, devon, salami, pies, pate and liverwurst), dairy foods and fats and oils. In total, these three food groups account for over 50 per cent of all fat that adults eat.

FIND THE FAT

Some fats are easy to cut down on. These include butter, margarine, oil, ghee, mayonnaise, cream, sour cream and the fat on meat and poultry. It is the fat hidden in foods that can contribute significantly to excess fat intake. Below is a basic guide to the fat content of foods, showing the amount contained in 100 g of each food (expressed as a percentage).

Negligible- or No-fat Foods

Bread, crispbread
Cereal foods – flours, meals, pasta, rice, porridge, breakfast cereals (except with coconut, nuts or oil)
Vegetables
Fruit (except avocado – 20% fat)
Egg white
Sugar, honey, jams, boiled sweets
Soft drink, cordial
Alcohol

Low-fat Foods (4% or less)

Most fish prepared without added fat – oysters, prawns, mussels, squid, crab, lobster, salmon, tuna (canned in water or fresh)
Chicken (skin and fat removed)
Very lean cuts of beef, veal, lamb and pork (prepared without added fat)
Modified milks – low-fat ('Shape') and reduced-fat ('Lite White', 'Hi-Lo', 'Rev', 'Skimmer')
Milk, full cream (3.8%)
Yoghurt – low-fat varieties
Low-fat cheese – cottage, ricotta
Water ices and gelato made without whole milk, cream or fat; ice confections

Medium-fat Foods (4 to 20%)

Meat – average lean cuts of beef, veal, lamb and pork
Egg and egg yolks
Biscuits – plain savoury and sweet (15%)
Cakes – plain and fruit cake (10-15%)
Buns, tea cakes – no cream (5-10%)
Ice cream (10%)

High-fat Foods (20 to 40%)

Fatty meat, luncheon meats and sausages
Fried food, particularly crumbed and battered foods
Pastry – puff and flaky (40%), shortcrust (30%), choux (20%)
Potato crisps and similar snack foods (25-35%)
Biscuits – chocolate, cream and shortbread types (25%)
Cakes – cream-filled and rich cakes (15% and over)
Cheese – cheddar, Edam, Swiss, Mozarella, Parmesan, Camembert, blue-vein, cream cheese (25-40%)
Cream (36%)
Sour cream (35%)
Coconut – fresh (35%), coconut cream (30%), coconut milk (25%)
Chocolate, carob confectionery (30%)

Very High Fat Foods (40 to 100%)

Vegetable oils, including olive oil and polyunsaturated oils (100%)
Hydrogenated coconut fat 'Copha' (100%)
Dripping, lard, ghee (99%)
Solid cooking and frying fats (99%)
Butter (80%)
Margarine – polyunsaturated, table, cooking (80%)
Nuts and nut butters (50-65%)
Mayonnaise (15-80%)
Fried bacon (40%)
Coconut – desiccated (65%), oil (100%)
Reduced-fat spreads (30-50%)

FAT IN YOUR DIET

Food group	Total percentage of fat intake
Meat, poultry and meat products	29.8
Dairy foods (excluding butter)	17.4
Fats (all non-cookery uses)	16.8
Grain products (bread, cereals, biscuits, cakes, pastry)	15.5
Vegetables	7.1
Nuts and seeds	3.0
Eggs	2.9
Condiments, flavourings and soups	2.9
Fish and seafood	1.5
All other foods	3.1
TOTAL	100.0

Source: Department of Community Services and Health (1987). National dietary survey of adults: 1983, No. 2, Nutrient intakes

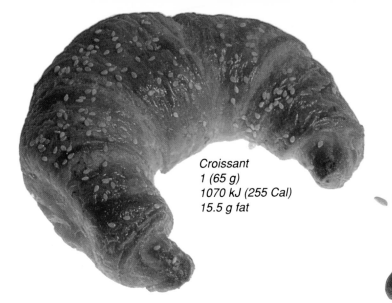

Croissant
1 (65 g)
1070 kJ (255 Cal)
15.5 g fat

Baklava
1 (105 g)
1620 kJ (385 Cal)
20 g fat

Toasted muesli
$^1/_2$ cup (30 g)
560 kJ (135 Cal)
6 g fat

Margarine and Butter
1 teaspoon (5 g)
150 kJ (35 Cal)
4 g fat

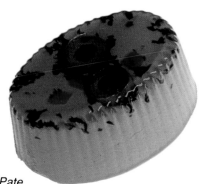

Pate
1 tablespoon (20 g)
250 kJ (60 Cal)
5 g fat

FATTY FAVOURITES

Check the quantity of fat contained in an average serve of the everyday foods pictured here. For a person consuming 7500 kilojoules (or 1800 Calories) a day, the recommended intake of fat should be no more than 60 g. This is based on 30 per cent of kilojoules (calories) being derived from fat.

Peanuts
50 g packet
1180 kJ (285 Cal)
24.5 g fat

Sesame bar
1 bar (50 g)
859 kJ (205 Cal)
15.5 g fat

Peanut butter
1 tablespoon (20 g)
520 kJ (125 Cal)
10.5 g fat

Mayonnaise
1 tablespoon (20 g)
590 kJ (145 Cal)
16 g fat

10 ways to cut fat in your cooking

Cutting fat and kilojoules is not as difficult as you think. Make it part of your everyday life.

1 Use as little oil, butter or margarine as possible when cooking. Avoid frying. Try grilling, dry-roasting on a rack, steaming, microwave cooking or wrapping in foil and baking. Barbecue on an open grill plate to allow fat to drip away.

2 Trim all visible fat from meat. Remove fat and skin from poultry. Shop for cuts of lean meat with the least fat and marbling, like round steak, fillet, rump, topside, leg of lamb, veal, pork fillet and leg steaks. Cut down on sausages, rissoles, bacon, luncheon meat and salami. A 500 g weight of meat will feed a family of four, especially with more vegetables and starchy foods.

3 Invest in a non-stick frypan and simply brush with a little oil before cooking – do not pour oil in. Over moderate (not high) heat, you can still brown and saute.

4 Stir-frying is an excellent way to prepare meals quickly and healthily. Just one tablespoon of oil in a pre-heated wok or deep pan can be used to stir-fry 2-3 cups of diced vegetables. Try cooking in stock for a different flavour.

5 Serve larger portions of low-fat starchy foods such as pasta, rice, potatoes, vegetables and dried beans and smaller portions of meat

WHAT CAN YOU DO?
Keep a record of what you eat over several days or a week to find out what foods are responsible for excess fat in your diet. Pay particular attention to fatty meat including sausages and luncheon meat, fatty chicken, full-cream dairy foods, rich biscuits and cakes, pies and pastries and fatty snack foods and takeaways; these foods are probably responsible for most of the fat in your diet.

6 Cook casseroles and soups a day ahead, chill overnight in the refrigerator. Any fat will solidify on the surface, making it easy to remove before heating.

7 Use low-fat or skim milk in cooking whenever possible. Try plain low-fat yoghurt in place of sour cream to finish casseroles (or half yoghurt, half sour cream). But do not reboil, as the yoghurt will curdle.

8 Marinate lean meat and chicken to improve tenderness and flavour. Try various combinations of aromatic spices and herbs with wine or low-salt soy sauce. Garlic, ginger, bay leaves, lemon rind, mustard, chilli, rosemary and five star spice are all delicious.

9 Be cautious with 'hidden fat' ingredients such as cheese, coconut, nuts, streaky bacon, chocolate and pastry and popular snacks such as biscuits, potato, crisps, cakes and buns.

10 For salads, modify the usual oil-and-vinegar dressing by simply diluting with water or making it with less oil. Avoid mayonnaise or mix mayonnaise with low-fat yoghurt and try no-oil commercial salad dressings.

LIGHTER AND LOWER

High-fat ingredient	Low-fat alternative
Cream	canned evaporated skim-milk, plain low-fat yoghurt, soft tofu, lightly beaten
Sour cream	plain low-fat yoghurt, buttermilk, soft tofu, lightly beaten with a squeeze of lemon juice
Cream cheese	ricotta cheese blended with a little caster sugar and vanilla essence
Butter, margarine	reduced-fat spread, reduce quantity of butter or margarine
Cheese (cheddar and other hard cheeses)	reduce quantity of cheese, half grated cheese, half breadcrumbs for toppings, half grated cheese half rolled oats for toppings
Coconut milk, coconut cream	canned evaporated skim milk or plain low-fat yoghurt mixed with 1-2 tablespoons desiccated coconut
Puff or shortcrust pastry	filo pastry, use half quantity of pastry - line bottom or top only

WHAT WE SAVED

10250 kilojoules (2450 Calories)
Fat   152 g
Cholesterol   110 mg
Sodium   2960 mg

LIGHT AND EASY

BEFORE

❖

APPLE PIE

- ☐ **500 g (1 lb) rich shortcrust pastry**
- ☐ **1 egg white, lightly beaten**

FILLING
- ☐ **7 large green apples, peeled and quartered**
- ☐ **$^1/_2$ cup (125 mL/4 fl.oz) water**
- ☐ **3 tablespoons honey**
- ☐ **3 tablespoons sultanas**
- ☐ **2 teaspoons grated lemon rind**
- ☐ **$^1/_4$ teaspoon allspice**

1   Roll out half the pastry to line a 23 cm (9 in) pie plate.
2   To make filling, cut apple quarters in half lengthways and place in a large saucepan with water, bring to the boil, reduce heat, cover and simmer for 5-8 minutes or until apples are just tender. Remove from heat and stir in honey, sultanas, lemon rind and allspice. Set aside to cool.
3   Spoon filling into pastry case. Brush edge of pastry with lightly beaten egg white. Roll out remaining pastry and cover filling. Make a decorative pattern around the edge.
4   Brush top of pie with egg white and sprinkle with sugar. Bake at 200°C (400°F) for 45 minutes or until pie is golden.

AFTER

❖

APPLE PIE

- ☐ **3 sheets filo pastry**
- ☐ **2 teaspoons polyunsaturated oil**

FILLING
- ☐ **7 large green apples, peeled and quartered**
- ☐ **$^1/_2$ cup (125 mL/4 fl.oz) water**
- ☐ **3 tablespoons honey**
- ☐ **3 tablespoons sultanas**
- ☐ **2 tablespoons grated lemon rind**
- ☐ **$^1/_4$ teaspoon allspice**

1   To make filling, cut apples in half lengthways and place in a large saucepan with water, bring to the boil, reduce heat and simmer for 5–8 minutes or until apples are just tender. Remove from heat and stir in honey, sultanas, lemon rind and allspice. Set aside to cool.
2   Brush sheets of filo with oil and stack. Place apple filling into a lightly greased 23 cm (9 in) pie plate and cover with filo pastry. Trim pastry, leaving 2.5 cm (1 in) edge around dish, and tuck under rim.
3   Decorate top of pie as desired. Bake at 180°C (350°F) for 30 minutes or until golden brown.

Breakfast In-the-bag

It's so easy to boost your nutrition with breakfast! Make a great start to the day with one of our easy breakfast ideas.

5 good reasons to enjoy your breakfast

1 Skipping meals, whether it's breakfast or any other meal, will make your total diet less satisfactory.

2 Breakfast skippers are more likely to 'break their fast' with sweet or fatty foods that are low in dietary fibre, such as potato crisps, pies, sausage rolls, sweet biscuits, cream buns and sugar-sweetened soft drinks.

3 Traditional breakfast foods such as cereals and bread are the main foods in your diet providing you with thiamin (vitamin B1) and complex carbohydrate (starch and dietary fibre). They are also good sources of iron, other B complex vitamins (niacin and riboflavin), protein, zinc and magnesium.

4 American studies have shown that people who have a cereal breakfast have lower blood cholesterol levels than breakfast skippers.

5 Preparing a healthy breakfast is just about the easiest job of the day. If you keep the right foods on hand, all your family (except the toddlers) can prepare their own.

Breakfast on-the-run

CEREALS – WHAT'S IN THEM?

As nature made them, cereals are wonderful foods – rich in starch and dietary fibre and a good source of many vitamins and minerals as well as protein. And this with no cholesterol, and little fat, sugar or sodium (salt).

Many processed cereal foods have kept the virtues of the original grain. Others have lots of added fat, sugar and salt, and some have lost a lot of their dietary fibre and some of their original vitamins in the refining process. Some cereal products have added fibre.

Look for the cereals with less fat, salt and sugar and more dietary fibre. Use our cereal guide as your standard.

Cereals of high nutritional quality: Rolled Oats; Cerola – Oat Bran Muesli; Kellogg's – Komplete Natural Muesli, Ready Wheats, Sustain; Uncle Toby's – True Swiss Formula Muesli and Willow Valley – Toasted Oat-bran.

Nutritious cereals but with more sodium than our standard: Kellogg's All Bran, and Bran Flakes; Sanitarium Weet-Bix; Uncle Toby's Vita Brits and Weeties.

YOUR CEREAL GUIDE

30 g ready-to-eat breakfast cereals

Energy	480 kJ
Protein	3 g
Fat	less than 2.5 g
Total carbohydrate	21 g
Sugars	less than 5.5 g
Dietary fibre	at least 1.9 g
Sodium	less than 36 mg

WHICH FIBRE?
▲ The fibre in wheat bran is mainly insoluble. Oat bran fibre is richer in soluble fibre. Rice bran fibre is a blend of both.
▲ Insoluble fibre helps prevent constipation. Soluble fibre helps to lower blood cholesterol levels in a low-fat diet.
▲ Use a variety of brans in your diet with a variety of wholegrain breads and cereals.

EGGS FOR BREAKFAST
Eggs for children. Use up to 1 egg each day in a low-fat diet.

Eggs for adults. Have your blood cholesterol level checked. If it is 5.2 millimoles or less, use up to 1 egg each day in your low-fat diet. If your blood cholesterol is more than 5 millimoles, restrict egg yolks to 3 or 4 weekly in your low-fat diet. For additional eggs use 'yolk-free egg mix'.

BREAKFAST ON-THE-RUN

If you don't have time to sit down for breakfast, pack yourself a tasty breakfast the night before and make sure you 'break your fast' with a healthy snack.

One Bag Full

2 or 3 crispbreads plain or lightly spread with polyunsaturated margarine or reduced-fat spread, a small quantity of reduced-fat cheese or cottage cheese and a piece of fresh fruit.

Two Bags Full

Dried fruit – apples, apricots, dates, figs, melon and raisins or sultanas – is always a popular choice and $1/3$ cup mixture of unsalted nuts and unsalted seeds like sunflower seeds.

Breakfast Box

2 slices wholemeal bread or 3 or 4 crispbreads spread lightly with polyunsaturated margarine or reduced-fat spread, 1 hard-boiled egg with a ripe tomato or piece of fruit.

EASY MICROWAVE ROLLED OATS

Follow the instructions on the pack or try our easy, no-fuss microwave method. For variety, add any of the following before cooking: chopped dried fruit, sesame seeds, sunflower seeds, oat bran, 1 or 2 teaspoons of instant skim milk powder for each serve of oats.

Serves 1

- ☐ **3 tablespoons rolled oats**
- ☐ **$1/2$ cup (125 mL/ 4 fl.oz) water**

Place oats and water in a microwave-safe bowl. Cover and cook on HIGH (100%) for 1-2 minutes, stir during cooking. Serve with hot or cold low-fat or reduced-fat milk.

460 kilojoules (110 Calories) per serve

Fat	2.5 g	medium
Cholesterol	none	
Fibre	3.0 g	medium
Sodium	1 mg	low

A BREAKFAST SHAKE

Serves 1

- ☐ **$1/2$ cup (125 mL/4fl.oz) reduced-fat or low fat milk**
- ☐ **3 tablespoons low-fat yoghurt, unflavoured or fruit**
- ☐ **1 piece fresh, soft ripe fruit or 3 tablespoons soft canned fruit**
- ☐ **1 tablespoon oat bran**
- ☐ **1 teaspoon sugar (optional) and not necessary when sweetened fruit yoghurt is used**

Place milk, yoghurt, fruit, bran and sugar in a food processor and process until smooth.

720 kilojoules (170 Calories) per serve

Fat	1.5 g	low
Cholesterol	7 mg	low
Fibre	3.0 g	medium
Sodium	120 mg	low

EASY BREAKFASTS

NO COOK
Try this combination for a simple 'no-cook' healthy breakfast.

- ▲ A piece of fresh fruit or fruit canned in light syrup or water.
- ▲ $1/2$-1 cup of ready-to-eat wholegrain breakfast cereal.
- ▲ Reduced- or low-fat milk with the cereal or as a drink.
- ▲ 1 or 2 slices of bread or toast, preferably wholegrain, with a scraping of polyunsaturated margarine or reduced-fat spread and a little jam or honey.
- ▲ Tea, coffee (use decaffeinated if you prefer) or milk.

SOMETHING HOT
When you want something hot to start the day, why not try porridge, baked beans on toast, toasted bread, muffins or crumpets with fresh sliced tomato and cheese or an egg cooked to order? If you are cutting down on cholesterol, substitute a sachet of 'yolk-free egg mix' for 2 eggs in your omelette or scrambled egg.

Lunch On-the-go

Ideas to help you enjoy that everyday takeaway meal you make yourself. Your lunch should be tasty and satisfying, it should include a variety of foods and supply about one-third of your daily nutrient needs.

PACK AND GO IDEAS

Don't skip lunch. You need it. Preparing lunch for school or work the night before will help avoid the morning rush. Encourage family members to help prepare their own.

△ Bread or bread rolls, preferably wholemeal.

△ Salad vegetables.

△ Lean meat, lean chicken, fish, eggs, cheese, peanut butter or baked beans.

△ Fresh, stewed or canned fruit or fruit juice.

△ Milk drink (low-fat or reduced-fat varieties) or yoghurt (low-fat unflavoured or flavoured varieties).

Every family can run short on ideas for everyday school lunches. Try these to tempt your children's tastebuds.

△ Sandwiches, rolls, individual packs of cheese, dried fruit and seeds like sunflower seeds.

△ Slices of raw vegetables such as carrots, capsicum, cucumber, mushrooms or celery to provide colour.

△ For a lunch box treat, pack meat-balls, cold chicken pieces, slices of meat loaf or a hard-boiled egg with a salad, bread roll, fruit juice and yoghurt.

△ In winter, use an insulated container or a vacuum flask for soups, stews or casseroles. Steaming home-made soup, a sandwich or roll and a piece of fruit make an excellent lunch.

△ In summer, salad boxes with various salads such as Waldorf, tabouli, potato or pasta and a variety of summer fruits, such as pineapple, strawberries and wedges of rockmelon.

Keep that summer lunch cool with frozen fruit pieces or fruit juices in a container. By lunchtime they will be thawed, but still refreshingly cold on a hot day.

For teenagers and those who need more food, muffins, scones and fruit loaf are ideal extras.

BRIGHT IDEAS WITHOUT BREAD

Here are some simple thoughts for sit-down lunches for days when you have more time – or plan to share your lunch hour with friends.

▲ Omelettes served with a salad and crispbreads. Crepes or pancakes with savoury fillings such as scrambled egg, baked beans or lentils, cottage cheese, creamed corn or savoury mince and vegetables.

▲ Use a variety of pastas, wholemeal and plain, combined with vegetables, tomato, lentil or bolognese sauce. Serve with salad.

▲ Rice combined with stir-fried vegetables and lean meat, chicken or fish and accompanied by a small amount of leftover vegetables, lean meats, chicken or fish.

▲ Hearty soups such as split pea, bean, minestrone, or vegetables and noodles served with croutons or bread rolls, or canned tomato soup made with skim milk and served with added canned beans.

▲ Rice cakes or crispbreads with cottage cheese and grated apple or peanut butter and celery.

IN THE OPEN

Choose a selection of open sandwiches to make a wonderful informal lunch for a group of people, or treat yourself to a favourite combination of fillings. If you use margarine, spread it very sparingly; if using a dressing or mayonnaise, there is no need to use margarine or a spread as well. There are many combinations of fresh ingredients you might like to try. It may inspire you to experiment with some combinations of your own.

Pack and Go Ideas

Avocado and Chicken on Pumpernickel, Smoked Salmon on Rye

AVOCADO AND CHICKEN ON PUMPERNICKEL

Makes 4 sandwiches

- ☐ 1 large avocado, peeled and seeded
- ☐ juice 1 lemon
- ☐ 155 g (5 oz) snow pea sprouts
- ☐ 4 slices pumpernickel bread
- ☐ fresh mint sprigs for garnish

CHICKEN SALAD
- ☐ 300 g (9¹/₂ oz) cooked chicken, chopped
- ☐ 2 shallots, finely chopped
- ☐ 1 tablespoon pine nuts
- ☐ 1 teaspoon chopped fresh mint
- ☐ 2 tablespoons light mayonnaise

1 Cut avocado into 12 slices and sprinkle with lemon juice.
2 To make chicken salad, combine chicken, shallots, pine nuts, mint and mayonnaise in a bowl.
3 Divide snow pea sprouts between bread slices and top with chicken salad. Arrange three avocado slices on top of chicken salad and garnish with mint sprigs.

1710 kilojoules (410 Calories) per serve
Fat	27 g	high
Cholesterol	100 mg	medium
Fibre	5.9 g	high
Sodium	340 mg	medium

SMOKED SALMON ON RYE

Makes 4 sandwiches

- ☐ 155 g (5 oz) thinly sliced smoked salmon
- ☐ 4 slices rye bread
- ☐ juice ¹/₂ lemon
- ☐ ¹/₂ red onion, cut into thin slices
- ☐ 8 thin slices cucumber
- ☐ 4 teaspoons drained capers
- ☐ 4 thin slices lemon
- ☐ freshly ground black pepper
- ☐ fresh dill sprigs for garnish

1 Arrange salmon on bread slices and sprinkle with a little lemon juice.
2 Place onion on salmon. Arrange cucumber, capers and lemon slices attractively on top. Season with plenty of freshly ground black pepper and garnish with dill sprigs. Serve with a tossed green salad.

600 kilojoules (145 Calories) per serve
Fat	4 g	medium
Cholesterol	26 mg	low
Fibre	3.8 g	medium
Sodium	1130 mg	high

Simply Sandwiches

Bring a little flair to a simple sandwich with our tempting suggestions for breads and fillings.

The sandwich is the simplest and most convenient way to make sure your family eats a nutritious lunch. Try different breads and fillings to bring a little variety into this traditional lunch.

BASICALLY BREAD

Use a variety of fresh breads, preferably wholemeal. Pocket breads can make fun sandwiches. Try mixing the sandwich with a combination of one slice wholemeal and one slice white. Make decker sandwiches with your favourite fillings. Use three slices of bread, such as one white slice with two wholemeal slices, and two fillings.

WHICH BREAD?

Whether wholemeal or white, bread is a nutritious food we all enjoy. In fact, health experts agree that we should be eating more.

Contrary to popular belief, bread is not fattening. It is low in fat and sugar and contains significant amounts of protein, vitamins, (especially thiamin), minerals, complex carbohydrates (starch) and dietary fibre. Wholemeal varieties contain more B-group vitamins and dietary fibre which makes them satisfying and helps keep the bowels regular. Read the labels and choose the low-salt or salt-reduced varieties.

There is a great variety of breads to choose. Why not try some of the following for snacks, lunch or dinner: crunchy bread rolls (horseshoe, long, round, with sesame or poppy seeds); bagels; English muffins or crumpets (try wholemeal and fruit varieties); French sticks and Vienna loaf; pita or pocket breads; Middle Eastern flat breads such as Lebanese and Turkish; raisin breads and fruit loaves; fruit buns; damper; rye and pumpernickel bread; Focaccia.

DID YOU KNOW?

Sandwiches were so called, the story goes, after the Fourth Earl of Sandwich (1718-1792). He apparently passed whole days in gambling. The waiter would bring him a piece of ham between two slices of bread, which he would eat without stopping play.

MIDDLE EASTERN POCKET SANDWICHES

Pita bread makes a wonderful container for holding all kinds of your favourite fillings. We have filled our pocket bread with refreshing cucumber salad, exotic lettuce leaves and succulent chunks of lean roast lamb.

Serves 4

- ☐ **4 wholemeal pita breads**
- ☐ **mignonette lettuce leaves**
- ☐ **400 g (12^1/$_2$ oz) lean roast lamb, cut into 1 cm (^{1}/$_2$ in) chunks**
- ☐ **fresh mint sprigs for garnish**

CUCUMBER AND YOGHURT SALAD
- ☐ **1 cucumber, peeled and chopped**
- ☐ **3 shallots, finely chopped**
- ☐ **^{1}/$_2$ cup (50 g) chopped fresh mint leaves**
- ☐ **200 mL (6^1/$_2$ fl.oz) low-fat unflavoured yoghurt**
- ☐ **1 tablespoon lemon juice**
- ☐ **^{1}/$_2$ teaspoon chilli sauce, or according to taste**
- ☐ **freshly ground black pepper**

1   Cut pita breads in half and carefully open. Line each half with lettuce leaves.
2   To make salad, place lamb, cucumber, shallots and mint in a bowl. Mix together yoghurt, lemon juice and chilli sauce. Pour over cucumber salad and fold gently to combine. Season with pepper.

1630 kilojoules (390 Calories) per serve

Fat	7.5 g	low
Cholesterol	112 mg	medium
Fibre	5.7 g	medium
Sodium	715 mg	high

KEEPING BREAD FRESH

Bread retains its freshness for three to four days when stored at room temperature in its original wrapping. If possible use a well-ventilated bread box or bin to store bread and clean it out regularly. In hot, humid weather keep your bread in the refrigerator.

For prolonged storage, keep bread in the freezer at temperatures between –18°C (0°F) and –25°C (–10°F). Most breads retain their original quality for up to four months. For best results, wrap and seal bread tightly then place on a wire rack in the freezer so that cold air can circulate freely and freeze it quickly. Freezing will not affect bread's nutritional value. Thaw bread at room temperature or in the microwave.

Because crusty breads dry out it is best to eat them on the day of baking.

TOASTED SANDWICHES

Try these fillings for toasted sandwiches. Butter one side of bread lightly if desired: baked beans with grated cheese; ham, cheese and tomato; savoury mince; tuna and cheese; cheese with pineapple; cream cheese (try the light variety) with sultanas. Toasted sandwiches can be made in a sandwich maker, under the grill or in the microwave using a preheated browning dish.

FILLING THOUGHTS

Spread bread or rolls sparingly with polyunsaturated margarine or butter (use the salt-reduced or low-salt varieties). Where soft moist fillings are used, like mayonnaise or cottage cheese, there is no need to use margarine or butter. Remember to choose the low-fat product wherever possible.

△ Ricotta or cottage cheese with: chopped apple and dates; grain mustard and well-drained asparagus; curry powder and sultanas; dried fruit (apricots) and walnuts.

△ Cheese (try the reduced-fat and reduced-salt varieties) grated or sliced with: grated carrot, lettuce and sultanas; gherkin; ham and pineapple; cucumber and alfalfa sprouts; tomato and lettuce.

△ Baked beans or bean mixes (no-added-salt, drained) with: lettuce and grated cheese; chopped ham; sliced onion and mushroom.

△ Chicken or turkey (remove skin) with: chopped celery and walnuts; shredded lettuce and cranberry sauce; light mayonnaise and celery.

△ Tuna, salmon or sardines with: alfalfa sprouts and sliced tomato; lettuce and onions; gherkin and light mayonnaise; cottage cheese and grated carrot.

△ Peanut butter (no-added-salt) with: chopped walnuts and lettuce; banana and raisins; grated carrot and alfalfa

WHAT'S IN IT?

White bread is made from white flour milled from wheat, it contains about 76 per cent of the wheat grain.

▲ Milk bread contains some added skim milk powder.

▲ Brown bread is made from at least 50 per cent wholemeal, the rest being white flour.

▲ Wholemeal bread is made from 90 per cent or more wholemeal flour.

▲ Protein-increased bread contains more protein than ordinary breads (ordinary breads contain about 9 per cent protein).

▲ Kibble wheat bread, sometimes labelled cracked or crushed wheat bread, may contain or be sprinkled with kibble or cracked grains. The fibre content is similar to brown bread (unless labelled 'wholemeal').

▲ Rye bread is made from a minimum of 30 per cent rye flour, the rest being white wheat flour.

sprouts; mushrooms and bean sprouts.

△ Hard-boiled egg, sliced or mashed with: grated cheese; cottage cheese and curry powder; lettuce and corn kernels; alfalfa sprouts and curry powder.

△ Sliced lean meat with: shredded lettuce and chutney; salad; potato salad; tomato and horseradish sauce.

△ Creamed corn with: chopped ham and lettuce; grated cheese; chives and radish.

Tasty Takeaways for School

Many children buy their lunch at school – it's fresh, reasonably priced and can be healthy

More teachers and parents are becoming aware of the importance of the school canteen in providing healthy and enjoyable foods which students can afford to buy.

The results of a 1988 Australian survey of school canteens (in New South Wales) showed that more schools, particularly primary schools, were not only switching to health canteens but that these canteens were popular and profitable!

PREPACKED LUNCHES

An easy way to provide a complete nutritionally balanced meal, is for the canteen to sell convenient packages. An example of a nutritionally balanced lunch pack would include: sandwich or roll with suitable filling; a piece of fresh fruit; milk drink or cheese stick/wedge. Other optional foods which could be included are: raw vegetable sticks; carton of yoghurt; hard-boiled egg; nuts and raisins.

Packed lunches should be varied to retain interest and proportioned to fit the appetites of different age groups. Here are some easy ideas:

△ Ham and cheese roll, apple, yoghurt.
△ Egg and lettuce sandwich, orange, milk drink.
△ Vegetable soup in a cup, cheese jaffle, fruit juice.
△ Salad-in-a-cup, buttered roll, cheese stick, banana.

TAKE A SNACK BREAK

Here are some tasty alternatives to the high-fat, sugar and salt snack foods commonly sold: corn cobs; dried fruit salad bags with puffed corn added; plain unsalted popcorn; muffin halves; small bags of unsalted nuts (not suitable for infants); raisin bread; wholemeal scones – plain, fruit, pumpkin or cheese; frozen fruit pieces; yoghurt, low-fat, unflavoured or flavoured; shredded wheatmeal biscuits with cheese; slices of fruit loaf; fruit smoothies (fruit, yoghurt and low-fat milk blended); vegetable snacks – carrot and celery sticks, celery boats filled with cottage cheese or peanut butter; fruit juice ice-blocks; fresh fruit; pikelets – plain or lightly spread with polyunsaturated margarine or butter.

HOT IDEAS

Why not try these ideas instead of hot pies and sausage rolls?

△ Toasted sandwiches – pop them in pie bags and reheat in the pie oven.
△ Hot potatoes baked in their jacket served with grated cheese, diced tomato or sweetcorn.
△ BBQ sausage in a wholemeal roll.
△ Hot soup in a mug.
△ Hot low-fat milk drinks.
△ Toasted meat sandwiches.
△ Hot rolls filled with cheese or savoury mince.
△ Meals in a cup – spaghetti bolognese, macaroni cheese.
△ Mini pizzas.
△ Healthy hot dogs for special occasions.
△ Healthy hamburgers for special occasions.
△ Toasted muffin and cheese.
△ Toasted raisin bread.
△ Meat balls on tooth picks.
△ Baked bean and cottage cheese toasted sandwich.
△ Fish fingers in a wholemeal roll.

CANTEEN GUIDELINES

▲ The canteen is important in the school education program as a practical example of the classroom sessions in nutrition and health.
▲ Be involved in the development of your children's school policy on what the canteen should provide for lunches and snacks.
▲ Follow the Healthy Diet Pyramid plan, which emphasises foods rich in complex carbohydrate, protein, vitamins and minerals and low in fat, sugar and salt.
▲ Encourage the sale of low-fat foods like sandwiches and bread rolls with low-fat fillings and salad and fruit as an alternative to pies, sausage rolls and fried foods.
▲ Introduce reduced-fat and low-fat milk drinks, yoghurt and cheese.
▲ As teachers and parents you can actively encourage students to make healthy food choices by involving them in the choices of foods to be sold.
▲ Have tasting sessions and special promotions – just like the local supermarket does!

❖

HAMBURGER

Serves 1

☐ 1 lettuce leaf
☐ 1 wholemeal roll, split and toasted
☐ 1 tablespoon bean sprouts
☐ 1 lean hamburger pattie
☐ 2 tomato slices
☐ 1 slice canned beetroot, drained
☐ 1 slice canned pineapple, in natural juice, drained
☐ freshly ground black pepper

Place lettuce on bottom half of roll and top with sprouts, pattie, tomato slices, beetroot and pineapple, season with pepper and top with remaining roll half.

1640 kilojoules (390 Calories) per serve

Fat	11 g	medium
Cholesterol	30 mg	low
Fibre	8.8 g	high
Sodium	800 mg	high

TACOS

Serves 6

- ☐ **125 g (4 oz) lean minced meat**
- ☐ **125 g (4 oz) canned red kidney beans**
- ☐ **freshly ground black pepper**
- ☐ **6 taco shells, heated**
- ☐ **shredded lettuce**
- ☐ **2 tomatoes, chopped**
- ☐ **60 g (2 oz) grated tasty cheese**

Cook meat in a non-stick frypan, stirring until browned, stir in beans and cook to heat through. Season with pepper. Divide meat mixture between taco shells and top with lettuce, tomato and cheese.

590 kilojoules (140 Calories) per serve

Fat	*7 g*	*high*
Cholesterol	*25 mg*	*low*
Fibre	*3.0 g*	*medium*
Sodium	*100 mg*	*low*

Mini Pizzas, Pita Burgers, Tacos

MINI PIZZAS

Serves 1

BASE
- ☐ **1 pocket pita bread, Lebanese bread, crumpet or half bread roll**

TOPPING
- ☐ **1 tablespoon tomato paste, no-added-salt**
- ☐ **pinch oregano**
- ☐ **1 tablespoon grated tasty cheese**

Choose from the following toppings:
- ☐ **1 tablespoon finely chopped ham**
- ☐ **4 tomato slices**
- ☐ **4 onion rings**
- ☐ **1 tablespoon pineapple pieces, drained**
- ☐ **2 tablespoons canned tuna, no-added-salt**
- ☐ **1 tablespoon chopped celery**
- ☐ **1 tablespoon cottage cheese**
- ☐ **1 tablespoon diced capsicum**
- ☐ **2 button mushrooms, sliced**

Spread base of your choice with tomato paste, then top with any other toppings you wish. Finally, sprinkle with oregano and top with cheese. Place under a preheated grill for 3-4 minutes or until cheese is melted and golden.

1470 kilojoules (350 Calories) per serve

Fat	*7 g*	*low*
Cholesterol	*36 mg*	*low*
Fibre	*5.2 g*	*medium*
Sodium	*800 mg*	*high*

PITA BURGERS

Serves 1

- ☐ **1 small pita bread round, heated**
- ☐ **1 lean hamburger pattie, cooked**
- ☐ **1 lettuce leaf**
- ☐ **1 tablespoon grated carrot**
- ☐ **1 tablespoon alfalfa sprouts**
- ☐ **2 tomato slices**
- ☐ **2 cucumber slices**
- ☐ **freshly ground black pepper**

Open out pita bread to form pocket and fill with pattie, lettuce, carrot, sprouts, tomato and cucumber. Season with pepper.

1400 kilojoules (330 Calories) per serve

Fat	*10 g*	*medium*
Cholesterol	*27 mg*	*low*
Fibre	*4.2 g*	*medium*
Sodium	*700 mg*	*high*

CHICKEN BURGER

Serves 1

- ☐ **2 tablespoons coleslaw**
- ☐ **1 wholemeal roll, split and toasted**
- ☐ **60 g (2 oz) diced lean chicken**
- ☐ **2 tomato slices**
- ☐ **freshly ground black pepper**

Place coleslaw on bottom half of roll and top with chicken and tomato slices, season with pepper and top with remaining roll.

1470 kilojoules (350 Calories) per serve

Fat	*8.5 g*	*medium*
Cholesterol	*80 mg*	*medium*
Fibre	*7.4 g*	*high*
Sodium	*570 mg*	*high*

Energy Food for Sport

You can't perform to your peak on the wrong food. Athletes and active people need more energy – and that means more carbohydrate.

MORE CARBOHYDRATE

Carbohydrate is present in the body as blood glucose (blood sugar). It is also stored as glycogen in the liver and muscles. Glycogen is made up of a number of units of glucose and is readily broken down to glucose when it is needed for energy. Glycogen is an important source of energy for the active person. When glycogen stored in the muscles run out, fatigue sets in and performance suffers.

Active people need a high carbohydrate diet (55 to 60 per cent of energy) to maintain adequate glycogen stores and blood sugar levels. Complex carbohydrate, mostly as starch, should provide the most carbohydrate.

REPLACING FLUIDS

Water is the best replacement fluid for active people (most electrolyte replacement drinks contain too much salt). Approximately 150-300 mL of fluid should be consumed for every 20-30 minutes of strenuous activity. Thirst is not a good indicator of fluid needs; active people need to drink more than their thirst dictates. Cold fluids (5-15°C) are best since they empty fastest from the stomach and keep the body cool.

Replace fluids regularly – don't wait until the end of a match or event when dehydration has set in.

STAY COOL

△ Exercise in the shade or at the coolest times of day.
△ Take it easy on hot days.
△ Wear light, loose-fitting clothing and a cap to allow the body to perspire freely.
△ Avoid exercise when you are ill or have a temperature.
△ If feeling overheated, fatigued or faint, **stop exercise.**

Food Boosters

The foods at right boost carbohydrate (mainly starch) and dietary fibre. The plant foods, grains or cereals and the foods made from them, vegetables, including the legumes (dried peas, beans and lentils) and fruits, are rich in carbohydrate and fibre and low in fat. Nuts and seeds also provide carbohydrate and fibre, but they are high-fat foods, the fats are mainly mono- or polyunsaturated.

D I D Y O U K N O W ?

Your body is 60 per cent water – when this percentage drops significantly, performance falters and heat stress is experienced.

CARBOHYDRATE-DIETARY FIBRE COUNTER

Food	Serve	Energy kJ (Cal)	Carbohydrate g	Fibre g
All-Bran	30 g	350(85)	22	9.3
apple	1 medium (170g)	390(95)	24	3.4
banana	1 medium (140g)	500(120)	28	3.5
baked beans	1 cup (165g)	445(105)	16	12.0
kidney beans, cooked	1 cup	790(190)	23	17.0
bread, white	1 slice (30g)	315(75)	14	0.8
bread, wholemeal	1 slice (30g)	270(65)	11	2.0
Corn Flakes	1 cup (30g)	460(110)	25	1.0
lentils, cooked	1 cup (165g)	690(165)	26	6.1
muesli (untoasted)	1/3 cup (30g)	415(100)	17	4.4
orange	1 medium (120g)	190(45)	10	3.1
orange juice	small glass	175(40)	9	0.4
pasta, cooked (white)	1 cup (200g)	925(220)	42	2.0
potato, boiled	1 medium	335(80)	16	1.3
rice, boiled white	1 cup (170g)	1110(265)	62	0.4
rice, boiled brown	1 cup (170g)	1145(275)	61	1.6
rolled-oats (cooked)	1 cup (250g)	470(110)	19	2.0
Weet-Bix	2 biscuits	400(95)	19	3.7

Source: Commonwealth Department of Community Services and Health 1989, NUTTAB version 89. Food industry data.

top tips for peak performance

Eat your pre-event meal about two to four hours before the competition. Choose foods you like. It's a good idea to experiment with different meals to find out what works best for you.

1 Top up your glycogen stores with high-carbohydrate foods.

2 Make that pre-event meal a low-fat occasion. Fat slows the digestive process.

3 Maintain hydration – drink a lot of fluids.

4 Prevent dehydration with no added salt. Excess salt will increase urine output.

5 Make a sober decision and avoid alcohol.

6 Try some of the 'shake-it-up' recipes – this way you can maintain your energy with liquid food.

Active Energy

A full schedule of study, work and training leaves little time for eating and sleeping. The following tips will help you maintain your active energy levels in record time.

▲ Keep nutritious snacks handy and try an extra snack on the way to and from training.

▲ Save on cooking time by cooking enough food for two meals, and freeze leftovers for another time.

▲ This table, which gives the kilojoule (calorie) equivalent of children's activities per 10 minutes, shows that energy output increases as body weight and the level of physical activity increases. This applies to adults and children. These are average figures and they will vary between individuals.

TOO HOT TO TROT?

Heat stress (hyperthermia) is a serious condition and severe cases may result in permanent physical damage and even death. Children and adolescents are more at risk of experiencing heat stress, because they have greater difficulty cooling their body down, particularly in very hot weather.

KILOJOULE (CALORIE) EQUIVALENTS OF CHILDREN'S ACTIVITIES

Activity Per 10 minutes	Body weight in kilograms			
	20-30 kg	*30-40 kg*	*40-50 kg*	*50-60 kg*
Sitting – resting	35-38 (8-9)	38-42 (9-10)	42-46 (10-11)	46-50 (11-12)
Walking 4 km/hr	70-90 (17-21)	90-110 (21-26)	110-125 (26-30)	125-145 (30-34)
6 km/hr	100-120 (24-28)	120-135 (28-32)	135-155 (32-37)	155-180 (37-43)
Tennis	90-140 (22-33)	140-185 (33-44)	185-230 (44-55)	230-280 (55-66)
Cycling 10 km/hr	65-85 (15-20)	85-110 (20-26)	110-140 (26-33)	140-165 (33-39)
15 km/hr	95-135 (22-32)	135-175 (32-41)	175-210 (41-50)	210-250 (50-60)
Soccer	150-225 (36-54)	225-300 (54-72)	300-380 (72-90)	380-455 (90-108)
Swimming – freestyle	105-155 (25-37)	155-205 (37-49)	205-260 (49-62)	260-310 (62-74)
Running 8 km/hr	155-220 (37-52)	220-280 (52-66)	280-330 (66-78)	330-380 (78-90)
10 km/hr	200-270 (48-64)	270-330 (64-79)	330-390 (79-92)	390-450 (92-107)
12 km/hr	– 320 (– 76)	320-385 (76-91)	385-450 (91-107)	450-515 (107-123)
14 km/hr	—	—	– 510 (– 121)	510-590 (121-140)
Squash	– 270 (– 64)	270-355 (64-85)	355-445 (85-106)	445-535 (106-127)

Source: Pediatric Sports Medicine 1983. Editor Oded Bar-Or. Springer-Verlag New York Inc.

The following recipes are high in carbohydrate and dietary fibre and low in fat. They are ideal for athletes and suitable for their less athletic friends, who would be better using smaller portions. Follow these main courses with fresh fruit, fruit salad or stewed or canned fruit. Serve fruit plain or with low-fat ice confection; low-fat yoghurt, unflavoured or fruit-flavoured; custard made with reduced-fat milk; rice cooked with dried fruit and reduced-fat milk; cottage cheese or ricotta cheese. Another suitable dessert course is dried fruit, unsalted nuts and seeds.

YOLK-FREE EGG MIX

We have used a yolk-free egg mix in several recipes in this book. It is a low cholesterol mix and is available as a frozen product from supermarkets. It is made from egg whites, polyunsaturated vegetable oil and skim milk and can be used in cooking in place of whole eggs. One sachet (100 g/3^1/2 oz) is the equivalent of two whole eggs. You might like to try using this mix in other recipes in place of eggs.

❖

SPEEDY TUNA SPAGHETTI

Serves 4

- ☐ **500 g (1 lb) spaghetti**
- ☐ **3 tablespoons finely chopped fresh parsley**

TUNA SAUCE
- ☐ **1 tablespoon polyunsaturated oil**
- ☐ **1 clove garlic, crushed**
- ☐ **1 onion, chopped**
- ☐ **125 g (4 oz) mushrooms, thinly sliced**
- ☐ **425 g (14 oz) canned tomatoes, undrained and mashed, no-added-salt**
- ☐ **90 g (3 oz) canned tuna, no-added-salt**
- ☐ **freshly ground pepper**

1 Cook spaghetti in boiling water following packet instructions. Drain and keep warm.
2 To make sauce, heat oil in a non-stick frypan and cook garlic and onion for 5 minutes or until onion softens.
2 Stir in mushrooms and cook for 5 minutes longer. Mix in tomatoes and simmer for 10 minutes. Add tuna, mix well and simmer uncovered for 10-12 minutes longer. Season to taste with pepper. To serve, spoon sauce over hot spaghetti and sprinkle with parsley.

2320 kilojoules (555 Calories) per serve
Fat	*7.5 g*	*low*
Cholesterol	*10 mg*	*low*
Fibre	*7.5 g*	*high*
Sodium	*42 mg*	*low*

❖

PORK AND BEANS

Serves 4

- ☐ **^{1}/2 cup (125 g/4 oz) raw haricot or butter beans**
- ☐ **1 tablespoon polyunsaturated margarine**
- ☐ **500 g (1 lb) diced lean pork**
- ☐ **2 carrots, cut into strips**
- ☐ **1 leek, roughly chopped**
- ☐ **2 cups (500 mL/16 fl.oz) vegetable stock, no-added-salt**
- ☐ **3 potatoes, peeled and cut into large cubes**
- ☐ **1 onion, sliced**
- ☐ **^{1}/4 small white cabbage, shredded**
- ☐ **^{1}/2 teaspoon dried thyme**
- ☐ **^{1}/4 teaspoon dried marjoram**

1 Soak haricot beans overnight, drain and cook in boiling water for 30 minutes. Drain and set aside.
2 Heat margarine in a non-stick frypan and stir-fry pork for 3-5 minutes or until browned. Transfer to a casserole dish, stir in haricot beans, carrots and leek.
3 Pour over stock, cover and cook at 180°C (350°F) for 50 minutes.
4 Add potatoes, onion, cabbage, thyme and marjoram and cook for 30 minutes longer.

1460 kilojoules (350 Calories) per serve
Fat	*7.0 g*	*low*
Cholesterol	*61 mg*	*medium*
Fibre	*13.6 g*	*high*
Sodium	*170 mg*	*low*

Speedy Tuna Spaghetti, Pork and Beans, Bean Curry

BEAN CURRY

This curry can be made with legumes of your choice. For a quicker version try making it using 425 g (14 oz) canned kidney beans. As these are already cooked it is just a matter of heating them through. Served with brown rice, a tossed salad and selection of sambals, this curry makes a great meal.

Serves 4

- [ ] **185 g (6 oz) raw butterbeans or other legumes**
- [ ] **1 tablespoon polyunsaturated oil**
- [ ] **1 large onion, quartered**
- [ ] **2 cloves garlic, crushed**
- [ ] **1 tablespoon chopped fresh ginger**
- [ ] **1 teaspoon ground cumin**
- [ ] **2 teaspoons ground coriander**
- [ ] **$^1/_4$ teaspoon ground cinnamon**
- [ ] **2 small hot chillies, seeds removed and chopped**
- [ ] **1 tablespoon plain flour**
- [ ] **$2^1/_2$ cups (600 mL/1 pt) water**
- [ ] **4 tomatoes, peeled and chopped**
- [ ] **1 tablespoon lemon or lime juice**
- [ ] **freshly ground pepper**

1 Soak beans overnight, drain and cook in boiling water for 1 hour or until beans are tender. Drain and set aside.

2 Heat oil in a non-stick pan and cook onion and garlic gently for 10 minutes or until onion begins to colour.

3 Add ginger, cumin, coriander, cinnamon and chillies and cook for 2-3 minutes longer. Stir in flour and cook for 1 minute longer. Mix in water and tomatoes and simmer for 10 minutes.

4 Add beans, lemon juice and pepper to taste and simmer for 10 minutes.

870 kilojoules (210 Calories) per serve

Fat	*6 g*	*medium*
Cholesterol	*none*	
Fibre	*14.4 g*	*high*
Sodium	*26 mg*	*low*

SAMBALS

The following sambals make great side dishes to have with Bean Curry.

▲ Sliced banana with lemon juice and coconut.

▲ Diced apple with chopped raisins and lemon juice.

▲ Thinly sliced unskinned cucumber in low-fat unflavoured yoghurt.

PASTA SURPRISE

Any type of small pasta, such as macaroni, can be used to make this interesting pasta bake. A 100 g sachet 'yolk-free egg mix' can be used in place of the eggs.

Serves 4

- ☐ 315 g (10 oz) wholemeal pasta
- ☐ 1 tablespoon polyunsaturated oil,
- ☐ 1 onion, chopped
- ☐ 6 large mushrooms, thinly sliced
- ☐ $^2/_3$ cup (100 g/$3^1/_2$ oz) sunflower seeds
- ☐ 2 eggs, beaten
- ☐ $^2/_3$ cup (185 g/6 oz) low-fat unflavoured yoghurt
- ☐ 1 cup (125 g/4 oz) reduced-fat, reduced-salt grated tasty cheese
- ☐ freshly ground black pepper, to taste
- ☐ 1 cup (60 g/2 oz) wholegrain bread crumbs

1   Cook pasta in boiling water following packet instructions. Drain and set aside.
2   Heat oil in a non-stick pan and cook onion, mushrooms and sunflower seeds for 5 minutes or until onion softens.

Remove from heat and stir in pasta, eggs, yoghurt and half the cheese. Season to taste with pepper.
3   Transfer to a lightly oiled ovenproof dish. Mix remaining cheese with breadcrumbs and sprinkle over pasta mixture. Bake at 180°C (350°F) for 30 minutes or until golden brown and firm.

2450 kilojoules (585 Calories) per serve

Fat	*25 g*	*high*
Cholesterol	*138 mg*	*medium*
Fibre	*13.3 g*	*high*
Sodium	*255 mg*	*high*

❖

MEXICAN STYLE BEEF

For a delicious family meal serve this spicy stew with brown rice, salad and wholemeal pita bread.

Serves 4

- ☐ 1 tablespoon polyunsaturated oil
- ☐ 2 onions, chopped
- ☐ 1 clove garlic, crushed
- ☐ 500 g (1 lb) lean topside, minced
- ☐ $^1/_2$ teaspoon chilli powder
- ☐ $^1/_2$ teaspoon ground cumin
- ☐ 2 tablespoons chopped fresh parsley
- ☐ 2 tablespoons tomato paste, no-added-salt
- ☐ 425 g (14 oz) canned tomatoes, no-added-salt, undrained and mashed
- ☐ 1 cup (250 mL/8 fl.oz) water
- ☐ 425 g (14 oz) canned kidney beans, no-added-salt, drained
- ☐ 425 g (14 oz) sweet corn kernels

1   Heat oil in a non-stick pan and cook onions and garlic gently until onions are golden.
2   Add mince and cook for 10 minutes or until brown, stirring to prevent meat clumping or burning. Stir in chilli powder, cumin, parsley, tomato paste, tomatoes and water. Cover and simmer for 1 hour.
3   Add beans and corn and cook over medium heat for 5 minutes longer.

1590 kilojoules (380 Calories) per serve

Fat	*11 g*	*medium*
Cholesterol	*73 mg*	*medium*
Fibre	*11.4 g*	*high*
Sodium	*315 mg*	*medium*

CHICKEN MACARONI

Serves 6

- ☐ 3 cups (500 g/1 lb) cooked pasta
- ☐ 250 g (8 oz) cooked chicken breast fillets, diced
- ☐ 425 g (14 oz) canned tomatoes, no-added-salt, undrained and mashed
- ☐ 2 sticks celery, chopped
- ☐ 1 green capsicum, chopped
- ☐ 2 carrots, chopped
- ☐ 2 shallots, chopped
- ☐ 3 tablespoons chopped fresh parsley
- ☐ freshly ground black pepper
- ☐ 1 cup (250 mL/4 fl.oz) stock

Combine pasta, chicken, tomatoes, celery, capsicum, carrots, shallots, parsley, pepper to taste and stock in a large ovenproof dish. Cover and bake at 180°C (350°F) for 30 minutes or until heated.

850 kilojoules (205 Calories) per serve

Fat	3 g	low
Cholesterol	38 mg	low
Fibre	7.4 g	high
Sodium	155 mg	low

POTATO HOTCAKES

Serves 4

- ☐ $1/2$ cup (60 g/2 oz) self-raising wholemeal flour, sifted
- ☐ 3 tablespoons low-fat milk
- ☐ 1 egg, lightly beaten
- ☐ 500 g (1 lb) potatoes, peeled and grated
- ☐ 1 small onion, finely chopped
- ☐ 1 small carrot, grated
- ☐ 1 tablespoon chopped fresh parsley
- ☐ freshly ground black pepper
- ☐ 2 teaspoons polyunsaturated oil

1 Blend flour, milk and egg together. Stir in potatoes, onion, carrot and parsley. Season to taste with pepper and mix well.
2 Heat oil in a non-stick frypan. Cover base of pan with a thin layer of mixture and flatten. Cook for 2 minutes, or until golden brown, then turn and cook other side for 2 minutes. Repeat with remaining mixture.

770 kilojoules (185 Calories) per serve

Fat	4.5g	medium
Cholesterol	57 mg	medium
Fibre	4.9 g	medium
Sodium	185 mg	low

FRUITY YOGHURT RICE CREAM

Serves 4

- ☐ $1^1/2$ cups (270 g/$8^1/2$ oz) cooked white or brown rice
- ☐ $1/2$ cup (125 g/4 oz) low-fat unflavoured yoghurt
- ☐ 1 tablespoon sugar
- ☐ 1 medium banana, thinly sliced
- ☐ pulp of 2 passionfruit

1 Combine rice, yoghurt, sugar, banana and passionfruit.
2 Spoon mixture into four individual ramekins and refrigerate until required.

700 kilojoules (170 Calories) per serve

Fat	1 g	low
Cholesterol	negligible	
Fibre	3.3 g	low
Sodium	28 mg	low

Left: Pasta Surprise, Mexican Style Beef
Below: Chicken Macaroni, Potato Hotcakes, Fruity Yoghurt Rice Cream

1   Heat oil in a non-stick pan and cook onions and garlic gently for 10 minutes or until onions are golden. Stir in ginger and curry powder and cook for 1-2 minutes longer.
2   Add tomatoes, lamb, lentils and water, cover and simmer for 40-50 minutes or until lamb is tender. Add more water during cooking if necessary.

1610 kilojoules (385 Calories) per serve

Fat	*10 g*	*medium*
Cholesterol	*82 mg*	*medium*
Fibre	*7.9 g*	*high*
Sodium	*120 mg*	*low*

BUBBLE AND SQUEAK

Serves 4

- [ ] **1 cup (185 g/6 oz) cold mashed potato**
- [ ] **220 g (7 oz) cooked, cold vegetables, cut into chunks**
- [ ] **1 small onion, chopped**
- [ ] **freshly ground black pepper**
- [ ] **2 teaspoons polyunsaturated oil**

1   Combine potato, vegetables and onion. Season to taste with pepper.
2   Heat oil in a non-stick frypan and spread potato mixture over base, cook until heated through and brown on the base.
4   Cut into four wedges and turn each wedge to brown on the other side.

340 kilojoules (80 Calories) per serve

Fat	*4 g*	*high*
Cholesterol	*negligible*	
Fibre	*3.2 g*	*medium*
Sodium	*80 mg*	*low*

NUTRITION TIPS

▲ Salads made from crispy, garden-fresh raw vegetables are an ideal way to keep the kilojoules down and the fibre up.
▲ Remember, fruit and vegetables come into the 'eat most' category when you are trying to maintain a nutritious diet while restricting fat.
▲ When steaming vegetables of different textures together, place the vegetables that take the longest time to cook on the bottom of the steamer, where they will cook more rapidly.

Above: Tuna and Rice Creole, Lamb and Lentil Hotpot
Right: Wholemeal Pikelets, Egg Flip, Milkshake, Smoothie

TUNA AND RICE CREOLE

Serves 4

- [ ] **1 cup (210 g/6¹/2 oz) brown rice, cooked**
- [ ] **3 shallots, chopped**
- [ ] **2 stalks celery, finely chopped**
- [ ] **1 carrot, grated**
- [ ] **1 red or green capsicum, sliced**
- [ ] **125 g (4 oz) mushrooms, sliced**
- [ ] **425 g (14 oz) tuna, no-added-salt, drained**
- [ ] **1 cup (125 g/4 oz) grated reduced-fat cheese**
- [ ] **1 cup (100 g/3¹/2 oz) rice bran**
- [ ] **2 tablespoons fresh parsley, chopped**
- [ ] **3 tablespoons lemon juice**
- [ ] **³/4 cup (190 mL/6 fl.oz) evaporated skim milk**
- [ ] **freshly ground black pepper, to taste**
- [ ] **2 large tomatoes, sliced**

1   Combine rice, shallots, celery, carrot, capsicum, mushrooms, tuna, cheese, rice bran, parsley, lemon juice and skim milk in a large mixing bowl and mix to combine. Season with pepper.

2   Spoon into a lightly greased ovenproof dish. Arrange tomatoes over tuna mixture and bake at 180°C (350°F) for 30-40 minutes.

2010 kilojoules (480 Calories) per serve

Fat	*15.5 g*	*medium*
Cholesterol	*70 mg*	*medium*
Fibre	*10.7 g*	*high*
Sodium	*465 mg*	*medium*

LAMB AND LENTIL HOTPOT

Serves 4

- [ ] **1 tablespoon polyunsaturated oil**
- [ ] **2 onions, chopped**
- [ ] **2 cloves garlic, crushed**
- [ ] **2 teaspoons chopped fresh ginger**
- [ ] **1 tablespoon curry powder**
- [ ] **2 large tomatoes, peeled and chopped**
- [ ] **500 g (1 lb) lamb, trimmed of all visible fat and cubed**
- [ ] **1 cup (200 g/6¹/2 oz) red lentils, washed and drained**
- [ ] **1 cup (250 mL/8 fl.oz) water**

SHAKE IT UP

BANANA SMOOTHIE

We have made our smoothie using full-cream milk, but it is just as good made with low-fat or fat-reduced milk.

Serves 2

- ☐ 1 cup (250 mL/8 fl.oz) milk
- ☐ 2 tablespoons skim milk powder
- ☐ 185 g (6 oz) low-fat banana yoghurt
- ☐ 2 bananas, chopped
- ☐ 2 thin orange slices
- ☐ nutmeg

Place milk, milk powder, yoghurt and bananas in a blender and blend until frothy. Pour into tall glasses and decorate with orange slices and a sprinkle of nutmeg. Serve chilled.

VARIATIONS

Rockmelon Racers: Substitute 125 g (4 oz) diced rockmelon for banana and use low-fat apricot or unflavoured yoghurt. Sprinkle top with cinnamon and serve in the empty rockmelon shell.

Strawberry Surprise: Substitute 125 g (4 oz) fresh strawberries for banana and use low-fat strawberry yoghurt. Decorate with a strawberry and serve in a long glass.

EGG FLIP

For breakfast on the run, try this nourishing meal in a glass. For a change, add a dash of your favourite fruit juice or nectar in place of the sugar and vanilla.

Serves 1

- ☐ 1 cup (250 mL/8 fl.oz) milk
- ☐ 2 tablespoons skim milk powder (optional)
- ☐ 1 egg
- ☐ vanilla essence
- ☐ sugar to taste
- ☐ nutmeg or cinnamon

Combine milk, milk powder, egg, vanilla and sugar in a blender and blend well. Pour into a tall glass and dust with cinnamon or nutmeg.

1310 kilojoules (310 Calories) per serve

Fat	15 g	high
Cholesterol	263 mg	high
Fibre	none	
Sodium	285 mg	medium

MILKSHAKE

The recipe below is for a basic milkshake. Try the following variations for a change. In place of the vanilla essence add 1-2 teaspoons instant coffee or 1-2 teaspoons drinking chocolate. For a fruity shake, add a piece of your favourite fruit or a dash of fruit juice.

- ☐ 1 cup (250 mL/8 fl.oz) milk
- ☐ 2 tablespoons skim milk powder (optional)
- ☐ 1 scoop vanilla ice cream
- ☐ vanilla essence
- ☐ sugar to taste

Place milk, milk powder, ice cream, vanilla and sugar in a blender and blend well. Pour into a long glass.

1357 kilojoules (325 Calories) per serve

Fat	13 g	high
Cholesterol	48 mg	low
Fibre	none	
Sodium	255 mg	medium

WHOLEMEAL PIKELETS

Makes 24 small or 12 medium pikelets

- ☐ 1 cup (135 g/4^{1}/2 oz) wholemeal self-raising flour
- ☐ 3/4 cup (190 mL/6 fl.oz) reduced-fat milk mixed with 1 teaspoon white vinegar or lemon juice
- ☐ 1 egg, beaten
- ☐ 2 tablespoons honey
- ☐ 1 tablespoon polyunsaturated oil

1   Sift flour and return grits to flour. Make a well in flour and pour in milk mixture, egg, honey and 2 teaspoons oil. Mix to combine thoroughly.

2   Heat remaining oil in non-stick frypan and drop a tablespoon of mixture at a time into pan. Cook until golden brown, turn and cook other side.

310 kilojoules (75 Calories) per serve

Fat	2.5 g	medium
Cholesterol	2 mg	low
Fibre	1.0 g	low
Sodium	115 mg	low

Full of Beans

Lentils, dried peas and beans (known collectively as pulses or legumes) have been part of man's staple diet since ancient times. They are a delicious and economical source of protein, fibre and other essential nutrients.

COOKING LEGUMES

All legumes except lentils and split peas require soaking before cooking. Soaking helps to clean and soften them. Soaking lentils and split peas will speed up the cooking time. Depending on how much time is available, legumes can either have a long or a short soak.

Do not salt cooking water as this causes the skins to split and the insides to toughen. The cooking time for legumes depends on type, age and quality. The fresher the beans, the shorter the cooking will be. All legumes should be brought to the boil and boiled rapidly for 5 minutes. Red kidney beans should be boiled for 10-15 minutes. The boiling kills toxins in the legumes.

Always cook legumes in a large pan with enough cold water to cover the legumes by 5 cm (2 in).

Long Soak

Rinse, then cover with cold water and leave at room temperature overnight. If soaking lentils or split peas only 10 minutes is needed. Drain and replace water before cooking.

Short Soak

Place the legumes in unsalted water and bring to the boil, then simmer for 5 minutes. Leave for 1-2 hours, then drain, rinse and use as required.

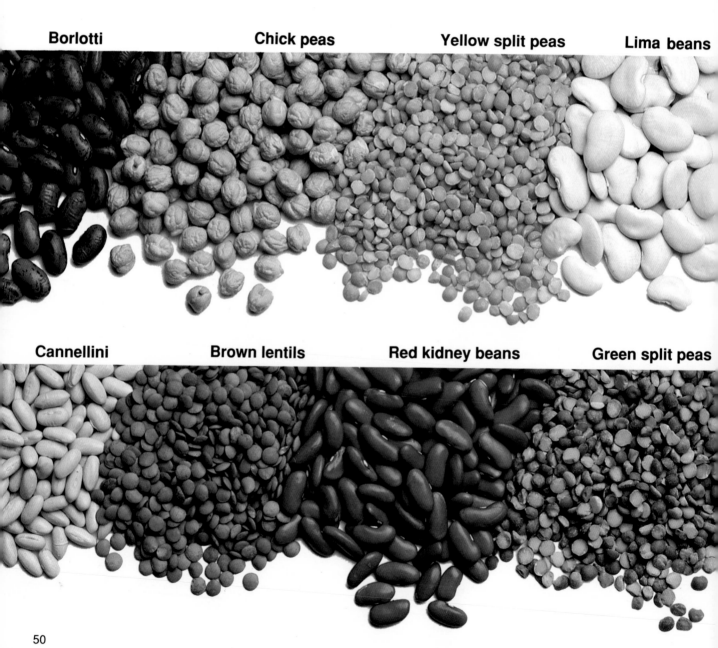

Borlotti   Chick peas   Yellow split peas   Lima beans

Cannellini   Brown lentils   Red kidney beans   Green split peas

LEGUME COOKING CHART

Legume	Short Soak Time	Cooking Time
Adzuki beans	1 hour	30-45 minutes
Black-eyed beans	1 hour	45 minutes-1 hour
Borlotti beans	1 hour	$1\frac{1}{4}$ hours-$1\frac{1}{2}$ hours
Butter beans	1 hour	1-$1\frac{1}{2}$ hours
Cannellini	1 hour	1-$1\frac{1}{2}$ hours
Chick peas	2 hours	1-$1\frac{1}{2}$ hours
Haricot beans	1 hour	1 hour
Lentils	—	30 minutes
Red kidney beans	1 hour	$1\frac{1}{4}$-$1\frac{1}{2}$ hours
Soya beans	2 hours	2-4 hours
Split peas	—	30 minutes

Soya beans   **Red lentils**   **Black-eyed beans**

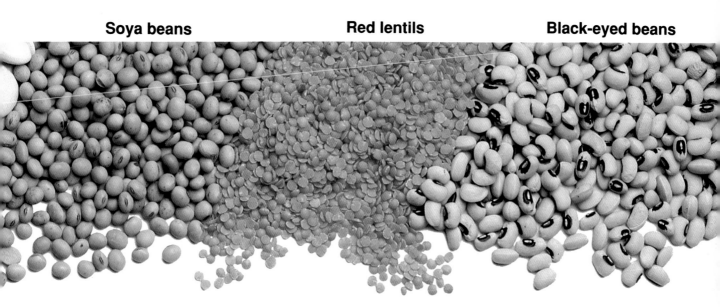

Haricot beans   **Adzuki beans**   **Yellow lentils**

Savour the Flavour

You'll discover how flavoursome food really is once you start to avoid salt and salted foods.

Salt has long been linked to hypertension or high blood pressure, a condition which, if unchecked, can lead to stroke, heart attack or kidney damage. Very small quantities of salt are essential for life. True physiological requirements are a mere 0.5 grams, which can easily be satisfied by the natural salt content of fresh foods. Studies of isolated tribal people who consume no added salt, such as the New Guinea Highlanders, Yanomamo Indians and Solomon Islanders, show that they have normal blood pressure throughout life. But once they adopt a Western eating pattern and lifestyle, some develop high blood pressure.

SALT IN YOUR DIET

The salt you add at home accounts for some 15-20 per cent of all your sodium intake. The salt used in commercial foods – estimated to be around 75 per cent of the total – is the real culprit. Common foods which do taste obviously salty like bread, butter, margarine, cheese, snack foods and processed meats (ham, devon, salami) contribute the most salt.

Another 10 per cent occurs naturally in our foods, with animal products like milk, eggs, meat and seafood containing more than vegetables, fruit or grains.

Although salt is the major source of sodium in our diet, others are bicarbonate of soda, MSG (mono-sodium glutamate) and sodium-based additives such as the preservative sodium metabisulphite.

Salt was once highly valued as a preserving agent. It allowed us to keep foods over the long winters and on journeys, when fresh food was scarce. Today, with our abundant food supply and modern processing techniques, there is virtually no need for salt-preserved foods.

DID YOU KNOW?

▲ Salt has been part of our culture for thousands of years. It is mentioned several times in the Bible – Lot's wife was turned into a pillar of salt when she looked backwards at the evil cities of Sodom and Gomorrah; Matthew preached to his followers: 'Ye are the salt of the earth'.

▲ In Roman times, soldiers were often paid in salt, called the *salarium argentum*, from which comes our word salary.

▲ Salt features in many religious customs. Bread and salt were once traditional offerings at weddings to ensure happiness and wealth; contracts were often solemnised with salt; anyone who spilled salt threw a pinch of it over the left shoulder to guard against evil.

SALT AND SWEAT

Many people believe that salt is essential in hot weather to replace that lost in sweat. The body, however, has very efficient mechanisms for conserving sodium and can maintain a fine balance between how much salt is eaten and the sodium dissolved in the sweat and urine. If you have cut out salt from your food, your sweat will be much less salty and more watery. After sweating, it is important to replace the lost water, not the sodium. Even athletes who undergo heavy sweating, for example, during a marathon run, do not need extra salt. Provided they are fully acclimatised and have been training in hot weather conditions, their sweat is much more dilute on a low-salt intake.

SALT IN YOUR FOOD

Classification of foods by salt content:

Low

Vegetables – fresh, frozen, dried, canned with no added salt
Fruit – fresh, frozen, dried, canned
Fruit juices
Plain flour, cornflour
Grains cooked without salt (rice, barley, millet, buckwheat, semolina, polenta)
Pasta
Legumes cooked without salt or canned without salt
Unprocessed wheat bran, oat bran, rice bran
Rolled oats cooked without salt, puffed wheat or rice cereals, breakfast cereals labelled no-added-salt, plain untoasted muesli
Nuts – unsalted
Ricotta or quark cheeses

Meat, fish, eggs, milk, yoghurt
Sugar, honey, jam, boiled sweets
Pure herbs and spices – fresh, dried
Oils
All products labelled salt-free or no-added-salt

Medium
Vegetables canned with salt
Salted nuts, hot potato chips
Cottage cheese
Sweet biscuits, cakes, pastries
Caramels, toffee, butterscotch
Some mineral waters (check label)
Breakfast cereals with more than 120 mg sodium per 100 g

High
Bread, cracker biscuits
Butter, margarine
Luncheon meats (devon, chicken loaf, meatwurst)
Pate, liverwurst, frankfurts
Soups – canned, packet
Cheese – firm cheeses (cheddar, Edam)
Canned tuna, salmon, sardines
Meat pies, sausage rolls, fried fast foods
Hamburgers, pizza
Chinese, Lebanese and Greek food
Electrolyte replacement sports drinks

Very High
Salt (including cooking salt, rock salt, sea salt and vegetable salt)
Meat tenderisers, meat seasonings
Stock cubes, stock powder, gravy powder
Yeast extract, meat extract
Anchovies, caviar, olives
MSG, soy sauce, most bottled sauces
Bacon, ham, corned beef, salami
Parmesan cheese, blue-vein cheese, cheese spread

SALT AND SODIUM
Salt is composed of sodium chloride. It is the sodium component that should be reduced. Our average intake of salt is currently estimated at two to three times more than the recommended intake. If we aim to cut sodium to one-third of what we are presently consuming, this will help prevent high blood pressure.

SALT CONTENT OF SAUCES AND DRESSINGS

Product	Salt content (%)	Sodium content mg per 100 g
Soy sauce, regular	18	7300
Soy sauce, reduced-salt	8	3000
Worcestershire sauce	4	1600
French dressing, regular	3.3	1330
Steak sauce	2.5-3.0	1000-12000
Tomato sauce, regular	2.5	1000
Tomato sauce, no-added-salt	0.09	35
Mayonnaise	1.9	750
Mayonnaise, no-added-salt	0.5	200
Coleslaw dressing	1.8	700
Italian dressing	1.7	660
Salad cream	1.5	600
Spicy tomato/plum sauce	0.8-1.5	300-600

Source: Manufacturers' analyses

DON'T ADD SALT
Do not add salt to food for your babies or children. While a desire for sweetness is innate, the liking for saltiness is not – it is acquired gradually after being introduced to foods with salt. Cow's milk, for example, contains three to four times more sodium than breast milk, which is just one of the reasons why it is unsuitable for babies.

A baby's kidneys have a poor capacity to eliminate sodium and cannot cope with salt. If excessive sodium is taken in, the baby can develop hypernatraemia (increased sodium levels in the blood) and suffer convulsions.

Commercial baby foods in the past contained salt to make the taste acceptable to parents, who were accustomed to sprinkling salt over their food. Today, baby foods are all made without any added salt and infant formulas are carefully formulated with as little sodium as possible.

SAUCES – CONDIMENTS
Avoid the trap of simply substituting sauces and condiments for flavour. Most sauces, seasonings, pickles, chutneys, dressings and mayonnaise are high in salt and will perpetuate your liking for a salty taste in your meals.

Soy sauce, fish sauce and oyster sauce, three common ingredients of Asian cuisine, contain around 18 per cent salt. Use small quantities of light salt-reduced soy sauce as an alternative, or else rely on the natural flavour or herbs and spices.

Worcestershire and similar brown sauces are more fruity than salty, but nevertheless contribute sodium and should be avoided or used sparingly. Commercial salad dressings and mayonnaise vary greatly in their salt content. It is best (and cheapest) to make your own at home or else shop for those labelled no-added-salt or salt-reduced.

HOW MUCH IS TOO MUCH?

Intake	salt g	sodium mg	millimoles*
Average	8-12	3200-4800	140-210
Recommended	2.3-6	920-2300	40-100
Requirement	0.5	200	10

* Sometimes the sodium is expressed as millimoles (mmol). Millimoles are calculated by dividing the milligrams by 23, the equivalent weight of sodium. The figures in the table are rounded off.

# easy steps to less salt

Avoiding the salt shaker and cooking without salt are essential first steps. However, this only reduces salt intake by a modest amount.

1 Stop sprinkling your food with salt. There is more than enough salt contained in everyday foods apart from the natural salt of fresh foods. Your taste buds will take three or four weeks to adjust to a lower salt level, so persevere and you will soon notice the true flavours of food unmasked by salt.

2 Stop cooking with salt. Recipes with salted ingredients such as stock powder or cubes, bacon, ham, soy sauce and cheese already include salt so you will not notice its absence. Others may need a flavour boost until your palate is accustomed to less salt.

3 Start buying salt-reduced or salt-free bread, rolls, crispbread, butter and polyunsaturated margarine. This will drop your salt intake significantly, particularly if you eat a lot of bread. Compare the difference per 100 grams:
▲ Regular butter and margarine: 2 per cent salt, 500 mg sodium
▲ Salt-reduced butter and margarine: 1 per cent salt, 400 mg sodium
▲ Salt-free butter and margarine: 0 per cent salt, less than 10 mg sodium

4 Never add salt to food for infants or children. They don't need it.

5 Pep up your cooking with the following aromatic ingredients:
▲ Herbs (fresh or dried) such as parsley, coriander, basil, oregano, rosemary, mint or thyme
▲ Oniony flavourings like onion, garlic, chives, spring onions
▲ Spices such as cinnamon, cardamom, cumin, nutmeg
▲ Hot flavourings like pepper, curry powder, chilli powder, fresh chilli, paprika
▲ Wine, sherry or small quantities of liqueurs
▲ Lemon or lime rind or juice, orange rind or juice, vinegar

6 Start shopping for low-salt, salt-reduced or no-added-salt varieties of your regular groceries. More and more products are available in a 'light' or salt-reduced form and often taste little different from their salted counterparts. Once you reduce the amount of salt you eat, you quickly notice how salty many foods taste and the thirst they create!

SALT SUBSTITUTES

A substitute can be helpful if you find unsalted food bland and unpalatable. It is helpful until your taste buds adjust. But as it still encourages a liking for a salty taste, you should view a salt substitute as a short-term 'aid'.

Potassium chloride is the most popular substitute for salt. A white crystalline powder, it can be sprinkled over food or added during manufacture. Fresh unsalted foods like vegetables, fruit and lean meat are rich in potassium.

Two types of salt substitute are available. One is composed only of potassium chloride. The other, a blend of potassium chloride and half sodium chloride, is only sodium reduced.

SALTY TALES

The many forms of salt (rock salt, sea salt and vegetable salt), are basically similar in composition and are still sodium chloride. None lowers your salt intake significantly.

Coarse rock salt is just as high in salt as the fine free-flowing table salt. It appears to produce a more intense salty flavour because the salt occurs in large chunks.
Sea salt is obtained by the evaporation of sea water and has around two-thirds the sodium of table salt.
Vegetable salt, celery salt, garlic salt and other herb salts contain some 70 per cent salt with dried ground vegetables, celery or garlic making up the remaining 30 per cent.

WHAT'S IN A NAME?

Low-salt foods should contain half the salt of the normal counterpart or no more than 120 mg sodium per 100 grams, whichever is the lower. This is the equivalent of 0.3 per cent salt.

Salt-reduced foods mostly claim to have one-third less salt than the usual product and are often labelled as 'light'. Examples include cheese, bread, lean ham, cracker biscuits and frozen ready-to-heat dinners.

Salt-free foods (often labelled 'no-added-salt') must not have salt added nor any ingredients containing salt.

Many manufacturers have also altered the formulation of ordinary products to contain less salt.

Handy Herb Guide

Use our table of suggested herb and spice combinations to enhance the flavour of your food. Herbs and spices contain virtually no sodium and can be used freely. But read the label of herb mixtures such as 'herb seasoning' or 'pepper blend', which can contain salt as an ingredient.

Vegetables	basil, caraway, chives, coriander, dill, fennel, garlic, marjoram, mustard, oregano, parsley, pepper, sage, thyme
Fish and shellfish	bay leaf, chives, dill, fennel, oregano, parsley, tarragon
Beef and veal	garlic, horseradish, juniper berries, marjoram, oregano, pepper, thyme
Lamb	coriander, marjoram, mint, rosemary
Pork	caraway, cumin, garlic, ginger, paprika, sage, thyme
Chicken and turkey	paprika, pepper, rosemary, sage, tarragon, thyme
Eggs	basil, caraway, chervil, chives, curry powder, paprika, sage
Breads and grains	caraway, chives, coriander, dill, dill seeds, marjoram, parsley, poppy seeds, sage, thyme
Fruit	allspice, cardamom, cinnamon, cloves, ginger, mint, nutmeg, vanilla

Basil

Sage

Chives

Dill

Parsley

Coriander

Rosemary

Oregano

Thyme

Mint

Snack Attack

Snacking is becoming more and more popular as lifestyles become busier. Variety is the key to healthy snacking.

Grazing or snacking on smaller meals frequently throughout the day is catching on around the world. The easy availability of fast foods, both from the supermarket and fast food outlets, makes grazing an easy option for busy people. It need not be a bad thing if done wisely. Well-planned snacks can include all the essential elements of a healthy diet.

When snacks are contributing a good proportion of the kilojoules in your diet, it is important that they are also a good source of other nutrients such as protein, vitamins and minerals. Unfortunately, it is all too easy to snack on foods that are high in kilojoules (calories), fat, sugar and salt, such as potato crisps, chocolate bars, sweet biscuits, cakes and pastries.

PROS AND CONS

△ Snacks are a useful way of filling in on kilojoules (calories) missed due to skipped meals.
△ Snacks and fast foods are convenient when you are busy.
△ Extra snacks top up the energy needs for growing children and sporting types.
△ Small, frequent snacks are ideal for people with poor appetites who cannot eat enough in three meals a day.
△ Snacks can become a liability if you eat more kilojoules than you need.
△ There is a tendency to overeat on quick and easy high kilojoule snacks and so be less hungry when the more nutrient-dense main meal arrives. Many children will not eat meals because they are too full of less nutritious snacks.
△ Many snack foods are sticky and sugary and if eaten alone, as snack foods usually are, can lead to dental decay.

WHO EATS SNACKS?

Everyone, at some time or other, relies on a snack to satisfy the appetite or simply be sociable.

Teenagers appear to be the most avid snackers, obtaining more of their total kilojoules from snacks than any other age group. A study of Australian (Sydney) students aged 15-16 years estimated that over 25 per cent of their daily kilojoules came from snacks. Reports from other parts of the world showed similar statistics.

The most common time for children and teenagers to eat snacks is after school. In a New York survey, 78 per cent of the teenagers interviewed ate snacks after school. This is the time, then, to have healthy snacks available at home. There may then be less temptation to buy a doughnut or soft drink on the way home from school.

Active children and adolescents often cannot supply all their energy needs from three meals a day, therefore snacks are an important extra source. They also should provide other important nutrients such as calcium, iron and various vitamins. Variety is the key to healthy snacking, as it is to healthy eating in general. (See the list of wise snacks.)

WISE SNACKS
Quick Snacks

Fresh fruit, frozen fruit pieces (orange quarters, banana halves, grapes)

Vegetable sticks (carrot, zucchini, capsicum) eaten alone or with a low-fat dip

Unsalted nuts, dried fruit (sultanas, dates, dried apricots), homemade popcorn (plain or flavoured with curry powder or other spices)

Hard-boiled egg, slice of cold lean meat, piece of cold cooked chicken (no skin), cold leftover rissole or slice of meatloaf

Slice or wedge of cheese, celery boats or pitted prunes filled with cottage cheese

Slice of wholemeal bread or crispbread spread with peanut butter or ricotta cheese, sandwich, pikelet, homemade muffin or scone, slice of fruit loaf

Glass of milk (try reduced-fat or skim and flavour with vanilla essence), milkshake or smoothie

Wholewheat breakfast biscuit with scrape of polyunsaturated margarine

Carton of yoghurt, plain or flavoured (try adding some chopped fresh fruit or spoonful of muesli to plain low-fat yoghurt)

Hot Snacks

Baked beans on toast, grilled cheese on toast, toasted sandwich, homemade soup (can be heated quickly in microwave)

FAST FOODS

Takeaway food is here to stay. To take advantage of its convenience and still maintain a healthy diet, it all comes down to being aware of the kinds of fast foods we eat and how often we eat them.

Extensive television advertising by fast food chains, aimed particularly at families and teenagers, has contributed to our increasing use of these foods.

Most people don't eat enough fast food to cause concern. However, some eat fast food regularly. The occasional takeaway in a varied diet is fine, but because these foods generally contain too much fat and salt and too little fibre, it is important to be aware of their contribution to the total diet.

When having a takeaway meal, try to finish with fresh fruit instead of the dessert and make sure the other meals of the day follow the Healthy Diet Pyramid plan.

FAT

The amount and type of fat in fast food can be a problem. Many are deep-fried in saturated fat, the type of fat which contributes to raised blood cholesterol levels.

The best way to avoid too much fat is to ask for food to be grilled instead of fried where possible, have barbecued chicken (remove the skin) instead of fried chicken, take the batter off the fish, and have smaller portions, adding some salad and fresh bread to fill the gap.

SALT

Salt is included in the cooking and then also added to most fast foods. The rolls, hamburger patties, sauces, pizza bases and toppings, chicken coatings and batters all contain salt. Then we add more. A fast food meal can supply more than half the maximum recommended amount (2300 mg) of sodium for an adult each day. It is very difficult to cut down on salt when eating takeaways, so ask for no extra salt to be added and remove the highly salted batters and coatings.

FIBRE

Many fast foods have very little dietary fibre. Ask for plenty of salad on your hamburger, have wholemeal rolls if available, and use the salad bar if there is one.

BEST FAST FOOD CHOICES

Freshly made wholemeal sandwiches and rolls
Hamburgers with lots of salad, on a wholemeal roll
Small pizza (best without the salami)

Kilojoules (calories)
Most takeaway foods come in large portions. They can supply up to half of the average kilojoule requirements of an adult and that is much more than is needed in any one meal. Often they are eaten as between-meal snacks. Fast food outlets usually do not provide many vegetables, fruits, or wholegrain cereal products to balance the meal. On their own most fast foods do not contain enough vitamins, minerals and fibre to balance the kilojoules.

WHAT'S IN FAST FOOD?

Food	Kilojoules (calories)	Fat (g)	Sodium (mg)
Meat pie (172 g)	1640 (390)	24	1030
Sausage roll (130 g)	1570 (375)	23	839
Hamburger, basic (170 g)	950 (225)	10	660
Chico Roll (170 g)	1670 (400)	18	900
Hot chips, salted (150 g)	1260 (300)	23	300
Fish, battered (140 g) no added salt	1490 (355)	22	160
Pizza, supreme (426 g)	4210 (1000)	47	2680
Pizza, ham and pineapple (404 g)	3990 (950)	40	2505
McDONALDS			
Big Mac (207 g)	2410 (575)	30	1097
Junior Burger (101 g)	1150 (275)	11	192
Cheeseburger (117 g)	1350 (320)	16	82
French fries (80 g) regular	860 (205)	12	122
PIZZA HUT			
Pizza, supreme (416 g)	4070 (970)	34	2080
Pizza, ham and pineapple (346 g)	3420 (815)	29	2214
KENTUCKY FRIED CHICKEN			
Snack box (264 g) (2 pieces chicken, mashed potato, gravy, bread roll)	2380 (565)	34	1240
Lunch pack (195 g) (1 piece chicken and French fries)	2350 (560)	35	440
Dinner box (432 g) (3 pieces chicken, mashed potato, gravy, coleslaw, bread roll)	3610 (860)	50	1850
CHINESE FOOD			
Chicken and almonds (200 g)	1150 (275)	20	860
Beef and blackbean sauce (200 g)	970 (230)	14	1120
Fried rice (200 g)	1490 (355)	14	800
Steamed rice (200 g)	720 (170)	0	10

The foods in this table are given in approximate serving sizes as purchased. The weight of each item is given in brackets so that comparisons can be made.

Sources:
1 McDonalds information leaflet
2 Metric Tables of Composition of Australian Foods, Thomas & Corden
3 Papers in the series 'Composition of Australian Foods' published in Food Technology in Australia (1980-82), authors Wills R.B.H., Greenfield, H. et al.

capsicum. Stir with spoon and cook for 2 minutes longer or until eggs are cooked but still moist. Spoon into pita halves and serve immediately with tomato wedges.

1130 kilojoules (270 Calories) per serve

Fat	15 g	high
Cholesterol	240 mg	high
Fibre	1.7 g	low
Sodium	415 mg	high

LENTIL SOUP

Serves 4

Make a pot of this tasty soup and store in the freezer in individual portions, ready for reheating in microwave.

- ☐ **1 teaspoon polyunsaturated oil**
- ☐ **1 onion, peeled and chopped**
- ☐ **1 carrot, peeled and chopped**
- ☐ **1 celery stick, chopped**
- ☐ **1 clove garlic, crushed**
- ☐ **125 g (4 oz) lentils, red or brown**
- ☐ **2 ¹/₂ cups (600 mL/1 pt) chicken stock or water**
- ☐ **1 tablespoon tomato paste**
- ☐ **freshly ground black pepper**
- ☐ **finely chopped parsley**

1   Heat oil in pan and cook onion, carrot, celery and garlic for 5 minutes or until vegetables are tender.
2   Stir in lentils, stock and tomato paste, bring to the boil, cover and simmer for 45 minutes, stirring occasionally. Season to taste with pepper. Just prior to serving, sprinkle with parsley.

570 kilojoules (135 Calories) per serve

Fat	1.5 g	low
Cholesterol	none	
Fibre	5.5 g	medium
Sodium	43 mg	low

NUTRITION TIP

▲ When compared by weight, the vegetable which is lowest in kilojoules (calories) is celery, followed closely by cucumber and lettuce. Three long sticks of celery, 20 lettuce leaves or ¹/₂ cucumber contain the same kilojoules (calories) as half a slice of bread and so are a great low-kilojoule snack.

SALMON RICOTTA DIP

Serve this delicious low-fat dip with vegetable sticks or spread on crackers.

Serves 8

- ☐ **2 cups (500 g/1 lb) ricotta cheese**
- ☐ **220 g (7 oz) canned salmon, no-added-salt, drained and flaked**
- ☐ **2 tablespoons chopped fresh parsley**
- ☐ **2 shallots, finely chopped**
- ☐ **1 stalk celery, chopped**
- ☐ **2 drops Tabasco sauce (optional)**
- ☐ **freshly ground black pepper**

Combine ricotta cheese, salmon, parsley, shallots, celery and Tabasco sauce in a bowl. Mix well and season to taste with pepper. Chill for 2-3 hours before serving.

530 kilojoules (130 Calories) per serve

Fat	8 g	high
Cholesterol	51 mg	medium
Fibre	negligible	
Sodium	158 mg	medium

SCRAMBLED SANDWICH

If you have no pita bread, try this mixture on wholemeal toast or an English muffin. Other flavourings you might like to try are finely chopped shallots or bean sprouts.

Serves 2

- ☐ **1 small pita bread round**
- ☐ **2 eggs, lightly beaten**
- ☐ **1 tablespoon reduced-fat milk**
- ☐ **freshly ground pepper**
- ☐ **2 teaspoons polyunsaturated margarine or butter**
- ☐ **¹/₄ cup (30 g/1 oz) grated cheese**
- ☐ **1 tablespoon corn kernels**
- ☐ **1 tablespoon chopped capsicum**
- ☐ **2 tomato wedges**

1   Cut pita bread in half. Beat eggs with milk and pepper in a small bowl. Melt margarine or butter in a small frypan. Pour in egg mixture and cook for 1 minute without stirring.
2   Sprinkle with cheese, corn and

CHICKEN SNACK

A quick snack which can be made in larger quantities and served with crusty bread as a light meal.

Serves 4

- [ ] **2 tablespoons low-fat unflavoured yoghurt**
- [ ] **1 teaspoon lemon juice**
- [ ] **¼ teaspoon curry powder**
- [ ] **125 g (4 oz) chopped cooked chicken**
- [ ] **½ small apple, cored and diced**
- [ ] **6 large grapes, halved**
- [ ] **4 lettuce leaves**

Combine yoghurt, lemon juice, curry powder, chicken, apple and grapes. Spoon into lettuce leaves.

290 kilojoules (70 Calories) per serve

Fat	1.5 g	low
Cholesterol	30 mg	low
Fibre	0.5 g	low
Sodium	30 mg	low

BANANA CINNAMON TOAST FINGERS

A sweet treat, great for afternoon snacking.

Serves 2

- [ ] **2 slices wholemeal bread, toasted**
- [ ] **2 teaspoons polyunsaturated margarine or butter**
- [ ] **2 bananas, cut into slices**
- [ ] **¼ teaspoon cinnamon**
- [ ] **1 teaspoon honey**

1 Spread toast with margarine. Place banana slices, cinnamon and honey in a mixing bowl, mash and spread over toast.

2 Place under a preheated grill for 2 minutes or until banana mixture bubbles. Cut into fingers and serve.

840 kilojoules (200 Calories) per serve

Fat	5 g	medium
Cholesterol	none	
Fibre	4.5 g	medium
Sodium	175 mg	medium

BEANS AND CHEESE

High-fibre, low-fat baked beans make a healthy snack at any time.

Serves 1

- [ ] **60 g (2 oz) canned baked beans, no-added-salt**
- [ ] **1 tablespoon finely chopped parsley**
- [ ] **1 slice wholemeal bread, toasted**
- [ ] **thin slice mozzarella cheese**

Combine beans and parsley and spread over toast. Top with cheese and place under a preheated grill until cheese melts.

760 kilojoules (185 Calories) per serve

Fat	7 g	medium
Cholesterol	18 mg	low
Fibre	6.7 g	high
Sodium	265 mg	medium

Scrambled Sandwich, Salmon Ricotta Dip, Chicken Snack

FROZEN FRUIT BLOCKS

These ice blocks are full of vitamins and fibre. Use whichever soft fruits are in season.

Makes 6 blocks

- ☐ ¹/2 cup (125 mL/4 fl.oz) fresh orange juice
- ☐ 1 medium apple, cored and quartered
- ☐ 1 medium orange, segmented
- ☐ 1 small banana, peeled and sliced
- ☐ paper cups or ice block containers
- ☐ wooden sticks

1 Place orange juice, apple, orange and banana in a food processor or blender and process until smooth.
2 Pour into containers and cover with foil. Make a slit in foil and insert wooden sticks. Freeze 5-6 hours or overnight.

130 kilojoules (30 Calories) per serve

Fat	negligible	
Cholesterol	none	
Fibre	1.0 g	low
Sodium	2 mg	low

CARROT AND SESAME MUFFINS

Delicious light muffins are perfect weekend fare. Any leftovers can be frozen and used when time is short.

Makes 12

- ☐ 3 cups (375 g/12 oz) self-raising flour
- ☐ ¹/2 teaspoon bicarbonate of soda
- ☐ 1 teaspoon mixed spice
- ☐ ¹/2 cup (90 g/3 oz) brown sugar
- ☐ 1 large carrot, grated
- ☐ 4 tablespoons toasted sesame seeds
- ☐ 1 cup (170 g/ 5¹/2 oz) sultanas
- ☐ 1 cup (250 g/8 oz) low-fat unflavoured yoghurt
- ☐ 1 cup (250 mL/8 fl.oz) skim or fat-reduced milk
- ☐ 3 tablespoons melted polyunsaturated margarine, salt-reduced
- ☐ 3 egg whites, lightly beaten

1 Sift flour, bicarbonate of soda and mixed spice into a mixing bowl. Add brown sugar, carrot, sesame seeds and sultanas.
2 Combine yoghurt, milk, margarine and egg whites and stir into flour mixture. Mix

until just combined. Spoon mixture into lightly greased muffin pans. Bake at 200°C (400°F) for 20 minutes or until golden brown.

588 kilojoules (139 Calories) per serve

Fat	4g	low
Cholesterol	none	
Fibre	1.2 g	medium
Sodium	214 mg	medium

CARROT AND PUMPKIN LOAF

This loaf can be cut into slices, wrapped and frozen for individual snacks or the school lunchbox.

Makes 1 loaf (20 slices)

- ☐ 3 tablespoons polyunsaturated vegetable oil
- ☐ 3 tablespoons brown sugar
- ☐ 1 egg
- ☐ 1 small carrot, grated
- ☐ 300 g pumpkin, cooked and mashed
- ☐ 1 cup (135 g/4¹/2 oz) plain wholemeal flour
- ☐ 1 cup (125 g/4 oz) plain flour
- ☐ 1 teaspoon bicarbonate of soda
- ☐ ¹/2 cup (90 g/3 oz) sultanas
- ☐ pinch each of nutmeg, cinnamon and ginger

1 Place oil and sugar in a mixing bowl and beat to combine. Beat in egg.
2 Fold in carrot and pumpkin. Sift together wholemeal and plain flours and bicarbonate of soda. Mix flour mixture, sultanas and spices into carrot mixture and mix well.
3 Pour into lightly greased 25 x 10 cm (10 x 4 in) loaf pan and bake at 180°C (350°F) for 1 hour or until cooked, when tested.

420 kilojoules (100 Calories) per slice

Fat	3.5 g	medium
Cholesterol	11 mg	low
Fibre	1.4 g	low
Sodium	43 mg	low

MICROWAVE IT

Hot drinks are quick and easy to make in the microwave. To make hot chocolate in the microwave, mix cocoa and sugar in a microwave-safe mug with a little hot water to dissolve cocoa, pour in milk and heat on HIGH (100%) for 1-1¹/2 minutes.

TROPICAL COOLER

This recipe makes enough for 10-12 large glasses and the fruit juice mixture can be stored in a covered container in the fridge to be used as required.

Serves 12

- ☐ 1 litre (1³/4 pt) orange juice
- ☐ 600 mL (1 pt) unsweetened pineapple juice
- ☐ ice cubes
- ☐ 1 litre (1³/4 pt) soda water
- ☐ mint leaves to decorate (optional)

1 Combine orange juice and pineapple juice in a large jug.
2 To serve, place ice cubes in a glass, half fill with fruit juice mixture and fill with soda water.

220 kilojoules (55 Calories) per serve

Fat	negligible	
Cholesterol	none	
Fibre	0.3 g	low
Sodium	9 mg	low

HOT CHOCOLATE DRINK

For a thicker fruity version of this delicious hot drink, blend half a banana into the milk before heating.

Serves 1

- ☐ 1 cup (250 mL/8 fl.oz) skim or reduced fat milk
- ☐ 1-2 teaspoons cocoa powder to taste
- ☐ 1 teaspoon sugar or honey

1 Place milk in a small saucepan and heat gently.
2 Mix cocoa and sugar or honey in mug with a little boiling water to dissolve and pour over hot milk.

660 kilojoules (160 Calories) per serve

Fat	4.5 g	medium
Cholesterol	20 mg	low
Fibre	1.0 g	low
Sodium	180 mg	low

Carrot and Pumpkin Loaf, Carrot and Sesame Muffins, Hot Chocolate Drink

Sweet Moderation

Sugar in small quantities can be part of a balanced diet. It adds flavour to foods and can be useful in cooking when preserving foods and browning bread and cakes.

Too much sugar can cause nutrition problems and this is the situation in Australia, for example, where refined sugar alone provides some 14 per cent of the kilojoules (calories) consumed.

Although sugar provides energy-giving carbohydrate, it contains no other essential nutrients for health – hence its description as an empty-kilojoule food. It is highly refined and easy to overconsume. Eaten in large amounts, it may displace more nutritious foods from your meals and create an unbalanced diet. It also plays a major role in the development of dental caries (tooth decay), especially if consumed between meals.

Many sugary foods such as desserts, chocolate, cakes and biscuits are also high in fat, making them high in kilojoules (calories). This is the main reason why they are restricted on weight-reducing and other diets where weight control is important, such as those designed for diabetics.

In developed countries, sugar consumption is approximately one kilogram of sugar per person per week. Yet it is difficult to notice how much sugar is actually eaten as most of this sugar intake is in the form of processed foods like sweetened soft drinks, cordial, confectionery, fruit drinks,

canned fruit, ice cream and breakfast cereals.

Today, around three-quarters of our sugar intake is consumed in the form of processed foods, while only one-quarter is consumed as sugar in the home, whether in tea and coffee or for cooking.

By contrast, at the turn of the century, most sugar was used at home in a variety of ways – to make puddings, cakes, biscuits, jams, bottled fruit and sweets – as well as for table use.

Sweetened soft drinks and confectionery are the largest users of sugar (beer and wine making also require a lot of sugar, but most of this is converted to alcohol). They are also the foods with the poorest food value and could be eliminated or reduced in your diet without any ill-effects.

HONEY OR SUGAR?

Honey is frequently promoted as a 'natural' alternative to sugar. And it is easy to see why! Being made by bees from the nectar of flowers and having a long history as both a food and medicinal agent certainly makes it an attractive foodstuff! Unfortunately, honey does not offer any special nutrition benefit over sugar. It contains some B vitamins and minerals but the

quantities are insignificant.

Honey is just as harmful to teeth as white sugar and provides kilojoules, like other sweet foods. It cannot be used as a sugar substitute on weight reduction or diabetic diets. So enjoy it as a pleasant sweetening agent but in limited amounts.

WHICH SUGAR?

Brown and raw sugar are often bought as healthier, more natural forms of sugar – an obvious conclusion if one is aware of the benefits of brown over white rice or brown (wholemeal) over white bread. However, in this case, colour is not a reliable guide to nutritional value. Brown and raw sugar have no health advantages over white, although they impart an attractive caramel flavour to dishes.

Brown sugar contains 85-95 per cent sucrose plus varying amounts of two other sugars – glucose and fructose. It is valued for its moistness in baking.

Raw sugar, with its chunky straw-coloured crystals, is virtually identical to white sugar and contains a similar 99 per cent sucrose.

Coffee crystals are formed from refined sugar syrup and have larger crystals, a darker colour and attractive flavour. Nutritionally they are the same as white sugar.

TOOTH CARE

Although the link between sugar and many health problems is now questionable, it is well accepted that sugar has a major role in the development of dental caries (tooth decay). All sugars can be broken down by bacteria present in the mouth to

form acids. These sugars include: sucrose (cane sugar), fructose and glucose (which occur in honey, fruit and vegetables together with sucrose), lactose (milk sugar), dextrose and maltose (breakdown products of starches produced during cooking or processing).

While any sugar has the potential to cause problems, sucrose or cane sugar plays the dominant role in the development of tooth decay because it is the most plentiful sugar in the average Western diet.

The acids produced by bacteria from sugar break down the mineral component of tooth enamel, causing it to erode and thus creating a cavity. The bacteria also convert some of the sugar to polysaccharides, which form a sticky film (plaque) over the surface of the teeth.

Frequency of sugar consumption and the form in which it is consumed are now held as more critical than the total amount eaten. Frequent sugary snacks between meals keep the tooth surface acid and are more cariogenic (caries-causing) than sugar consumed with meals.

Sticky sweet foods – such as chewy lollies, sticky cakes or muesli bars – which cling to the surface of the teeth and take a long time to clear from the mouth are particularly damaging. Sugar dissolved in drinks, however, clears through the mouth quickly and is less harmful.

In addition, the flow and composition of saliva, the level of fluoride in drinking water, other anti-cariogenic factors in foods and individual susceptibility to cavities are other factors which come into play.

While you cannot alter the teeth you were born with, you can help keep them in top condition by regular cleaning and by following the guidelines for good nutrition. Food that is good for your body is also the best for your teeth! It is not necessary to eliminate sugar completely from your diet to prevent tooth decay. Just steer clear of sweet snacks between meals, especially if they are sticky and chewy, and try to clean teeth as soon as possible after eating sweets.

Fruit and vegetables certainly contain a variety of sugars which can be converted to acid in the mouth by bacteria. They also contain other valuable nutrients such as vitamins, minerals and fibre – which are necessary for good health and are therefore nutritionally important.

Some people mistakenly believe that substituting honey, golden syrup or molasses for table sugar will prevent tooth decay. But these foods contain high concentrations of sugars which can still be broken by bacteria in the mouth. Thus they are just as cariogenic as ordinary sugar. Many so-called 'health bars' sweetened with honey or syrup are very cariogenic, being sticky and clinging to the teeth.

DIABETES AND SUGAR

Diabetes is frequently believed to be caused by too much sugar. In fact, it was formerly called 'sugar diabetes', which attests to the perceived relationship between sugar and the disturbance in blood sugar levels that occurs with diabetes.

In the past, the main dietary treatment has been to avoid sugar completely and restrict the amount of starchy carbohydrate consumed. As a result, diabetics tended to eat a low-carbohydrate diet with lots of fat (from additional meat, cheese, eggs, fats and oils), which only served to increase their risk of coronary complications later in life.

Today, nutritionists agree that sugar is not a direct cause of diabetes and that other lifestyle factors, such as being overweight or inactive are more important determinants. Excess weight arises from consuming too many kilojoules (calories) generally and doing too little exercise. Naturally, if sugar contributes to those extra kilojoules, then it is an indirect cause of diabetes, but so are many other foods if consumed over and above daily needs.

The recommended diet for people with diabetes is a low-fat, high-starch, high-fibre diet. With such a plan, fats are minimised which benefits the heart, while starchy high-fibre carbohydrates tend to be digested slowly, so avoiding peaks in blood glucose levels. Legumes are extremely effective and should be included as often as possible.

Providing the person is not overweight and the diabetes is well controlled, small amounts of sugar taken with a fibre-rich meal can be part of a diabetic's food intake. In addition to weight control, maintaining an even spacing of carbohydrate at each meal remains a vital part of diabetic control. For these reasons, a visit to a trained dietitian is vital to have the best type of food plan. If you are still following a low-carbohydrate diet, now is the time to have it re-evaluated.

Just Desserts

Whatever sugary substance you favour, avoid those bad-for-you, in-between sweet snacks. Why not wait and indulge instead in some of our delightful, healthy desserts?

❖

FRUITY KEBABS WITH RASPBERRY SAUCE

An easy, barbecued dessert that is sure to please all the children in your family – big and small. The sauce is optional, but is really too delicious not to include. For a change you might like to make it with strawberries, boysenberries or blackberries.

Serves 4

☐ **3 ripe medium bananas, cut into 2 cm (³/4 in) pieces**
☐ **juice of ¹/2 lemon**
☐ **2 kiwifruit, cut into 2 cm (³/4 in) pieces**

RASPBERRY SAUCE
☐ **1 punnet (250 g/8 oz) raspberries**
☐ **juice of 1 orange**
☐ **1 teaspoon caster sugar**

1 To make sauce, place raspberries, orange juice and sugar in a food processor or blender. Process until smooth, press through a sieve and discard raspberry seeds. Refrigerate until ready to serve.
2 Place bananas in a mixing bowl with a few drops of lemon juice and toss to coat. Thread banana and kiwifruit pieces alternately onto oiled wooden skewers.
3 Cook kebabs on a hot barbecue or under a preheated grill for 4-5 minutes and turn once during cooking. To serve, spoon chilled raspberry sauce over the warm kebabs.

470 kilojoules (110 Calories) per serve
Fat	negligible	
Cholesterol	none	
Fibre	6.65 g	high
Sodium	negligible	

❖

APRICOT AND CHERRY CRUMBLE

A rather special Spring dessert when made with fresh fruit, but also delicious when canned fruit is used. When using canned fruit, choose the unsweetened varieties and of course there will be no need to precook the apricots.

Serves 6

☐ **9 fresh ripe apricots, washed, halved and stones removed**
☐ **2 tablespoons water**
☐ **1 tablespoon sugar**
☐ **250 g (8 oz) fresh cherries, stones removed**

TOPPING
☐ **¹/2 cup (45 g/1¹/2 oz) rolled oats**
☐ **1 tablespoon plain wholemeal flour**
☐ **1 tablespoon desiccated coconut**
☐ **2 tablespoons chopped almonds**
☐ **1 tablespoon honey**
☐ **1 tablespoon polyunsaturated margarine or butter**

1 Place apricots and water in a deep ovenproof dish and sprinkle with sugar. Bake at 180°C (350°F) for 15 minutes.
2 To make topping, place rolled oats, flour, coconut, almonds and honey in a bowl and rub through margarine, until mixture resembles breadcrumbs.
3 Top apricots with cherries and sprinkle with topping mixture. Bake at 180°C (350°F) for 10-15 minutes or until golden.

620 kilojoules (145 Calories) per serve
Fat	6 g	medium
Cholesterol	none	
Fibre	3.8 g	medium
Sodium	26 mg	low

Fruity Kebabs with Raspberry Sauce, Apricot and Cherry Crumble, Baked Apple with Prunes

BAKED APPLE WITH PRUNES

A popular dessert with children. They will enjoy helping you make it as much as eating it. Baked apples are also delicious eaten cold, making ideal lunch box or picnic food.

Serves 1

- [ ] **1 large apple, cored**
- [ ] **2 almonds, chopped**
- [ ] **1 dried apricot, chopped**
- [ ] **2 prunes**
- [ ] **1 tablespoon water**
- [ ] **1 teaspoon brown sugar**

1   Make a shallow horizontal cut in the skin around the centre of the apple – this prevents it bursting during cooking. Place apple in a small ovenproof dish and fill the hole with almonds, apricot and prunes. Pour water over apple and sprinkle with sugar.

2   Bake at 180°C (350°F) for 30-50 minutes or until apple is tender. The cooking time depends on the size and variety of the apple used. Serve hot with the cooking juices.

750 kilojoules (180 Calories) per serve

Fat	6.5 g	medium
Cholesterol	none	
Fibre	7.8 g	high
Sodium	8 mg	low

DID YOU KNOW?

▲ Apples were gathered by Stone Age man and were cultivated by the ancient Greeks, Romans and Egyptians.

▲ There are more than 7000 varieties of apples in the world today.

▲ If peeled apples are soaked in cold water with a tablespoon of lemon juice for 15 minutes they remain pale when cooked.

▲ Apples team well with many other fruits, especially plums, quinces and apricots.

▲ Dessert apples have a firm juicy flesh and may be eaten on their own or make an interesting finish to a meal when served with a variety of cheeses.

▲ The easiest way to neatly slice apples is to first core them, then peel, halve and finally cut them into even slices.

DID YOU KNOW?

▲ Pears are a member of the rose family and have been cultivated in Europe since ancient times.

▲ Keep pears in a cool place and check them daily as they ripen very quickly. Overripe pears are tasteless and woolly.

▲ Pears are ready to eat when they have a subtle scent and will yield to slight pressure at the stalk.

POLENTA AND APPLE FLAN

This easy-to-prepare flan of apples and polenta custard is delicious served hot or cold. Polenta is a maize flour much used in Italy for both savoury and sweet dishes. It is available in most supermarkets, Italian food stores and health-food shops. The grainy texture of cooked polenta may surprise you at first, but that's how it's meant to be. If you wish, you can halve the quantity of polenta used.

Serves 8

- ☐ **4 green apples, cored, peeled and sliced**
- ☐ **1 tablespoon caster sugar**
- ☐ **1 teaspoon finely grated lemon rind**

POLENTA CUSTARD
- ☐ **1¹/₂ cups (375 mL/12 fl.oz) low-fat milk**
- ☐ **2¹/₂ tablespoons polenta**
- ☐ **1 tablespoon caster sugar**
- ☐ **¹/₂ teaspoon vanilla essence**
- ☐ **2 tablespoons sultanas**

1   Combine apples, sugar and lemon rind. Place in a lightly greased shallow ovenproof dish. Cover and bake at 220°C (425°F) for 15 minutes or until apples are tender.

2   To make polenta custard, blend 3 tablespoons milk with polenta. Heat remaining milk in a saucepan, stir in polenta mixture, sugar, vanilla essence and sultanas. Bring to the boil over a medium heat, stirring, until mixture thickens.

3   Pour polenta custard over cooked apples and bake at 220°C (425°F) for 10 minutes or until custard sets.

380 kilojoules (90 Calories) per serve

Fat	negligible	
Cholesterol	negligible	
Fibre	1.6 g	low
Sodium	30 mg	low

AUTUMN SOUFFLE

In Autumn, when apples and pears are at their best, transform them into this wonderfully light souffle. Popular with the whole family, it is the perfect dessert to top off a heavier meal.

Makes 4 individual souffles

- ☐ **1 pear, peeled and cut into small pieces**
- ☐ **1 Granny Smith apple, cored, peeled and cut into small pieces**
- ☐ **1 teaspoon lemon juice**
- ☐ **1 tablespoon water**
- ☐ **1 tablespoon caster sugar**
- ☐ **¹/₄ teaspoon vanilla essence**
- ☐ **4 egg whites**
- ☐ **2 tablespoons icing sugar**

1   Place pear and apple in a small saucepan, add lemon juice and water. Cover and cook for 10 minutes or until fruit softens.

2   Mash or blend fruit to a fine puree. Stir in 1¹/₂ teaspoons sugar and cook over low heat for 2 minutes, stirring to evaporate a little moisture from the fruit. Place puree in a mixing bowl and stir in vanilla essence.

3   Beat egg whites until soft peaks form, add remaining sugar and continue beating until whites are stiff.

4   Mix 2 tablespoons beaten egg white into fruit puree then gently fold in remaining whites. Spoon souffle mixture into lightly greased individual souffle dishes, flattening the top gently with a knife. Place on an oven tray and bake at 180°C (350°F) for 12-15 minutes. Dust tops of souffles with icing sugar and serve immediately.

390 kilojoules (95 Calories) per serve

Fat	none	
Cholesterol	none	
Fibre	1.4 g	low
Sodium	60 mg	low

Above: Autumn Souffle
Right: Pear and Apricot Pancakes, Tropical Sago Pudding

PEAR AND APRICOT PANCAKES

'Pancake' is a magic word full of beautiful childhood memories. These pancakes are delicious served hot, cold or warm.

Serves 4

- ☐ 4 tablespoons plain wholemeal flour
- ☐ 3 tablespoons plain flour
- ☐ 1 egg
- ☐ 1 tablespoon honey, warmed
- ☐ a pinch ground cinnamon
- ☐ 1/2 cup (125 mL/4 fl.oz) skim milk
- ☐ 1 large pear, peeled, halved and finely chopped
- ☐ 1 teaspoon polyunsaturated margarine or butter, melted
- ☐ 1 teaspoon polyunsaturated oil
- ☐ 2 tablespoons apricot jam

1   Sift wholemeal and plain flours into a large mixing bowl and make a well in the centre. Combine egg, honey, cinnamon and milk, pour into the flour and mix well. Fold through pear and margarine.

2   Heat a non-stick frypan and brush with a little oil. Pour in enough pancake and pear batter to cover the base of pan. Cook until brown on each side. Repeat with remaining mixture. Spread pancakes with jam and garnish with pear slices if desired.

690 kilojoules (165 Calories) per serve

Fat	4 g	medium
Cholesterol	57 mg	medium
Fibre	2.1 g	medium
Sodium	45 mg	low

❖

TROPICAL SAGO PUDDING

This filling dessert is ideal to serve after a light main meal.

Serves 6

- ☐ 3 tablespoons sago soaked in 1/2 cup (125 mL/4 fl.oz) water
- ☐ 1 1/2 cups (375 mL/12 fl.oz) low-fat milk
- ☐ 1 tablespoon honey
- ☐ 1 cup (315 g/10 oz) fresh pineapple, diced
- ☐ 3 tablespoons diced dried pawpaw
- ☐ 1/2 teaspoon vanilla essence
- ☐ 1 tablespoon desiccated coconut
- ☐ pulp 2 passionfruit

1   Place sago mixture, milk and honey in a saucepan and bring to the boil, stirring constantly. Cook for 10-15 minutes or until mixture thickens and sago softens and becomes transparent. Add more water if mixture becomes too thick during cooking.

2   Stir in pineapple, pawpaw, vanilla essence and coconut and cook for 1 minute longer. Pour into a deep dish or individual souffle dishes and allow to cool. Refrigerate until set and ready to serve. Top with passionfruit pulp just prior to serving.

410 kilojoules (100 Calories) per serve

Fat	1 g	low
Cholesterol	negligible	
Fibre	4.0 g	medium
Sodium	negligible	

SAGO

Sago is a starchy food which is extracted from palm trees in tropical areas. Pacific Islanders and South-East Asians use it to thicken soups and for making desserts and puddings. South Americans and Europeans may be more familiar with tapioca, a similar food that can act as a substitute for sago.

STRAWBERRY SAUCE

Many fresh fruits can be transformed into smooth, sweet and flavoursome sauces to serve with baked and fresh fruits, pancakes, souffles, fruit kebabs, cakes and puddings. They can easily be frozen and used to replace cream or ice cream. Use the following recipe as a guide to making other fruit sauces such as mango, apricot or raspberry sauce. Simply replace the strawberries with the same quantity of your chosen fruit.

Serves 6

- ☐ **juice of 1 orange**
- ☐ **juice of 1 lemon**
- ☐ **1 tablespoon sugar**
- ☐ **250 g (8 oz) strawberries, hulled**

Place orange juice, lemon juice, sugar and strawberries in a food processor or blender and process until smooth. Refrigerate until required.

120 kilojoules (30 Calories) per serve

Fat	none	
Cholesterol	none	
Fibre	1.0 g	low
Sodium	negligible	

❖

WINTER FRUIT SALAD

Make this colourful salad in Winter when oranges and mandarins are at their best.

Serves 4

- ☐ **³/₄ cup (185 mL/6 fl.oz) fresh orange juice**
- ☐ **2 tablespoons raisins**
- ☐ **1 tablespoon brandy (optional)**
- ☐ **1 tablespoon honey**
- ☐ **1 orange, peeled and segmented**
- ☐ **6 mandarins, peeled and segmented**
- ☐ **3 tablespoons flaked almonds, roughly chopped**

1   Combine orange juice, raisins, brandy and honey in a glass bowl. Fold through orange and mandarin segments.
2   Cover and refrigerate until required. Remove from refrigerator 20 minutes before serving. Just prior to serving sprinkle with almonds.

630 kilojoules (150 Calories) per serve

Fat	4 g	medium
Cholesterol	none	
Fibre	4.3 g	medium
Sodium	9 mg	low

EASY AND HEALTHY

The following dessert suggestions are quick to prepare and healthy to eat.

FRUIT PARFAITS

Serves 4

- ☐ **¹/₂ small honeydew, seeds removed**
- ☐ **250 g (8 oz) strawberries, hulled and halved**
- ☐ **1 banana, mashed**
- ☐ **¹/₂ cup (125 g/4 oz) low-fat unflavoured yoghurt**
- ☐ **pinch nutmeg**

Scoop flesh from the melon using a melon baller. Divide strawberries and melon balls between four parfait glasses. Reserve a few strawberry halves for garnish. Combine banana, yoghurt and nutmeg and spoon over fruit. Top with reserved strawberries.

FRUIT DIP

Serves 6

- ☐ **250 g (8 oz) low-fat unflavoured yoghurt**
- ☐ **¹/₂ teaspoon ground cinnamon**
- ☐ **3 tablespoons fruit jam**
- ☐ **selection fresh fruit, to serve**

Mix together yoghurt, cinnamon and jam. Cover and refrigerate. To serve, spoon into an attractive bowl and serve with a platter of fresh fruit.

❖

EXOTIC FRUIT LOAF

This moist fruit loaf contains no added sugar or fat. It is delicious served as a dessert with a fruit sauce.

12 Slices

- ☐ **15 dried pear halves**
- ☐ **10 dried apricots**
- ☐ **2 cups (500 mL/16 fl.oz) water**
- ☐ **1 ripe banana**
- ☐ **1¹/₂ cups (200 g/6¹/₂ oz) wholemeal self-raising flour**
- ☐ **60 g (2 oz) chopped almonds**
- ☐ **60 g (2 oz) dried pawpaw, chopped**
- ☐ **60 g (2 oz) dried mango, chopped**
- ☐ **¹/₄ teaspoon cinnamon**

1   Place pears, apricots and water in a saucepan, bring to the boil, cover and simmer for 5 minutes. Remove pears with a slotted spoon and set aside. Place apricots, cooking liquid and banana in a food processor or blender and process until smooth.
2   Pour fruit mixture into a large mixing bowl and stir in flour, almonds, pawpaw, mango and cinnamon. Spoon a quarter of the mixture into a very lightly greased and lined 25 x 10 cm (10 x 4 in) loaf pan. Top with a third of the pears. Repeat layers until all mixture and pears are used, ending with a layer of mixture.
3   Bake at 180°C (350°F) for 50 minutes or until cooked when tested. Stand loaf in pan for 5 minutes before turning onto a wire rack to cool.

620 kilojoules (150 Calories) per slice

Fat	3 g	low
Cholesterol	none	
Fibre	6.5 g	high
Sodium	160 mg	low

❖

CREAMY FRESH STRAWBERRY YOGHURT

We have made this dessert using strawberries, but you might like to try it using other fresh fruits such as bananas, mango or apricots.

Serves 4

- ☐ **220 g (7 oz) low-fat unflavoured yoghurt**
- ☐ **2 tablespoons milk**
- ☐ **1 tablespoon sugar**
- ☐ **125 g (4 oz) strawberries, hulled and quartered**

Place yoghurt and milk in a mixing bowl and beat for 5 minutes or until light and smooth. Gently fold through sugar and strawberries. Refrigerate until required.

300 kilojoules (70 Calories) per serve

Fat	1.5 g	low
Cholesterol	6 mg	low
Fibre	1.1 g	low
Sodium	50 mg	low

Winter Fruit Salad, Creamy Fresh Strawberry Yoghurt, Exotic Fruit Loaf

HONEY AND LEMON CREPES

In these crepes we replaced the milk with tea. We have served our crepes warm with lemon juice and honey but you might like to serve them with a fruit filling, or they can be used as a savoury crepe.

Serves 4

CREPES
- ☐ **100 g (3¹/₂ oz) plain flour, sifted**
- ☐ **1 egg, beaten**
- ☐ **1 cup (250 mL/8 fl.oz) cold tea**

TOPPING
- ☐ **4 teaspoons lemon juice**
- ☐ **4 tablespoons honey, warmed**

1   To make crepes, place flour in a bowl and make a well in the centre. Add egg and work flour in from the sides. Stir in tea a little at a time to make a smooth batter of pouring consistency. Set aside to stand for 30 minutes before cooking.
2   Pour 2 tablespoons batter into a lightly greased non-stick frypan. Cook pancakes until golden each side. To serve, stack pancakes and top with honey and lemon juice.

880 kilojoules (210 Calories) per serve

Fat	7 g	medium
Cholesterol	55 mg	medium
Fibre	1.0 g	low
Sodium	20 mg	low

SUMMER BERRY JELLY

This beautiful and easy-to-make jelly is set with agar-agar, an edible sea vegetable gelatine which is popular in Asia.

Serves 4

- ☐ **1¹/₂ cups (375 mL/12 fl.oz) fresh orange juice**
- ☐ **250 g (8 oz) strawberries, halved**
- ☐ **1 tablespoon agar-agar**
- ☐ **125 g (4 oz) blueberries**
- ☐ **125 g (4 oz) blackberries**

1   Place orange juice, 200 g strawberries and agar-agar in a saucepan. Bring to the boil and simmer for 5 minutes or until strawberries soften. Push mixture through a sieve and discard seeds.
2   Place blueberries and remaining strawberries and strawberry liquid in a food processor or blender and process until smooth. Rinse mould in cold water and pour in berry mixture. Allow to cool then refrigerate until set.
3   To unmould jelly, dip the mould in a little lukewarm water. Place a plate on top of mould and quickly turn over. A little shake may be necessary to separate the jelly from the mould.

350 kilojoules (85 Calories) per serve

Fat	negligible	
Cholesterol	none	
Fibre	5.0 g	medium
Sodium	7 mg	low

Summer Berry Jelly

CARROT CASSATA ROLL

This carrot roll makes a surprising change from the better known carrot cake. The cassata filling makes it the perfect finish to a special dinner.

Serves 8

- ☐ **4 eggs, separated**
- ☐ **$^1/_2$ cup (125 g/4 oz) caster sugar**
- ☐ **$^1/_2$ cup (60 g/2 oz) plain flour**
- ☐ **1 teaspoon ground cinnamon**
- ☐ **1 teaspoon ground nutmeg**
- ☐ **1 teaspoon ground allspice**
- ☐ **1 large carrot, grated**
- ☐ **2 tablespoons golden syrup**
- ☐ **icing sugar, sifted**

FILLING
- ☐ **2 tablespoons finely chopped preserved ginger**
- ☐ **125 g (4 oz) dried fruit salad mix, finely chopped**
- ☐ **$^1/_2$ cup (125 mL/4 fl.oz) dark rum**
- ☐ **250 g (8 oz) ricotta or cottage cheese**
- ☐ **125 g (4 oz) low-fat unflavoured yoghurt**
- ☐ **1 tablespoon honey**
- ☐ **1 teaspoon ground nutmeg**

1   Beat egg yolks with sugar until pale and thick. Sift together flour, cinnamon, nutmeg and allspice and fold through egg yolks with carrot. Beat egg whites until soft peaks form. Gradually add golden syrup and continue to beat until stiff. Fold through carrot mixture.

2   Spoon batter carefully into a greased 30 x 25 cm (12 x 10 in) Swiss roll pan lined with baking paper. Cook in a preheated oven at 180°C (350°F) for 15-20 minutes or until firm to touch.

3   When roll is cooked, turn out quickly onto a sheet of baking paper sprinkled with caster sugar and roll up from the short end like a Swiss roll. Stand until cold.

4   To make filling, soak ginger and fruit salad mix in rum for at least 1 hour. In food processor or blender, process ricotta, yoghurt, honey and nutmeg. Drain fruit mixture and fold through ricotta mixture.

5   Unroll cake when cold, and remove baking paper. Spread with filling and re-roll. To serve, sprinkle with icing sugar and cut into slices.

1170 kilojoules (255 Calories) per serve

Fat	*3.5 g*	*low*
Cholesterol	*118 mg*	*medium*
Fibre	*1.8 g*	*low*
Sodium	*125 mg*	*low*

CARAMEL BREAD PUDDING

This bread pudding is a delicious adaptation of an old favourite.

Serves 6

- ☐ **200 g (6$^1/_2$ oz) yolk free egg mix, thawed**
- ☐ **1 tablespoon golden syrup**
- ☐ **3 tablespoons brown sugar**
- ☐ **1 teaspoon vanilla essence**
- ☐ **1$^1/_2$ cups (375 mL/12 fl.oz) low-fat milk**
- ☐ **1$^1/_2$ cups (375 mL/12 fl.oz) evaporated skim milk**
- ☐ **6 slices stale wholemeal bread, crusts removed**
- ☐ **1 tablespoon polyunsaturated margarine**
- ☐ **1 tablespoon sultanas**
- ☐ **$^1/_4$ teaspoon cinnamon**

1   Whisk egg mix, golden syrup, 1 tablespoon sugar and vanilla essence together in a bowl, then whisk in low-fat and evaporated milks gradually.

2   Spread each slice of bread sparingly with margarine and cut into fingers. Place a layer of bread in the base of an ovenproof dish, sprinkle with sultanas and pour over half the milk mixture. Set aside to stand for 10 minutes.

3   Top with remaining bread and pour over remaining milk mixture. Sift remaining sugar and cinnamon over the top of the custard.

4   Stand dish in a baking pan and carefully pour in enough boiling water to come halfway up the sides. Bake at 180°C (350°F) for 40 minutes or until set.

1110 kilojoules (265 Calories) per serve

Fat	*7.5 g*	*medium*
Cholesterol	*negligible*	
Fibre	*1.9 g*	*low*
Sodium	*350 mg*	*medium*

LIGHT AND EASY

CREAMY APRICOT CHEESECAKE

Serves 8

BASE
- ☐ **125 g (4 oz) sweet biscuit crumbs**
- ☐ **1 tablespoon ground almonds**
- ☐ **60 g (2 oz) polyunsaturated margarine or butter**

FILLING
- ☐ **250 g (8 oz) ricotta cheese**
- ☐ **125 g (4 oz) cottage cheese**
- ☐ **1 tablespoon fine semolina**
- ☐ **2 tablespoons low-fat apricot yoghurt**
- ☐ **3 eggs, separated**
- ☐ **³/4 cup (185 g/6 oz) caster sugar**
- ☐ **2 teaspoons grated lemon rind**
- ☐ **4 canned apricot halves, in natural juice, drained and chopped**

1 To make base, combine biscuit crumbs, almonds and margarine. Spread over the base of a lightly greased 20 cm (8 in) springform pan and set aside.
2 To make filling, place ricotta cheese, cottage cheese, semolina, yoghurt and egg yolks in a food processor or blender and process until smooth.
3 Beat egg whites until soft peaks form. Add sugar a spoonful at a time, beating well after each addition until whites are thick and glossy.
4 Fold cheese mixture into egg whites, then lightly fold through lemon rind and apricots. Spoon mixture into prepared pan and bake at 180°C (350°F) for 50-55 minutes or until firm. Cool in pan.

1380 kilojoules (320 Calories) per serve

Fat	*14 g*	*high*
Cholesterol	*100 mg*	*medium*
Fibre	*1.0 g*	*low*
Sodium	*220 mg*	*medium*

HOW WE'VE CUT FAT AND KILOJOULES

▲ Instead of the usual cream cheese or cream cheese and yoghurt combination, we have used ricotta cheese with cottage cheese and folded in beaten egg white to create a smooth creamy texture.

▲ Our base has just enough margarine to bind the biscuit crumbs. In its place you could use a sponge layer or low-fat pastry if preferred.

▲ Semolina thickens and sets the cake, reducing the need for another egg, so saving kilojoules.

7 easy ways to reduce your sugar intake

1 Forget sweetened soft drinks and cordial. Quench your thirst with iced water, vegetable juices, diluted fruit juices, plain mineral water, soda water or low-joule soft drinks.

2 Reduce your intake of sugary foods such as lollies, chocolate, biscuits, cakes and jams.

3 Gradually reduce the amount of sugar added to drinks and cereals.

4 Try to buy low-sugar varieties of foods. Choose fruit canned in juice or in light syrup rather than in heavy syrup; low-sugar cereals; plain sweet biscuits instead of fancy, iced ones.

5 Try not to finish every meal with 'something sweet'. Like salt, your taste buds will become accustomed to less and less sugar, but it takes a little time. Why not follow a main meal with a simple fresh green salad, or a fresh fruit platter?

6 Experiment with less sugar or honey in recipes. Many recipes can have one-quarter or one-third less sugar, and still turn out successfully.

7 Read ingredient labels carefully. The proportion of sugar in a food is indicated by its order on the list of ingredients – if sugar is one of the first three ingredients stated, the food is likely to have a high content of sugar.

BUY LESS SUGAR

It is important to understand the food label. Every time you shop, you no doubt see food labels which say 'no-added-sugar', 'unsweetened' or 'low-joule food'. Do these all mean the same thing?

No-added-sugar often appears on the label of fruit juice, canned fruit or cereal. It means that the product contains no added sugars such as cane sugar, glucose, fructose or lactose, nor does it contain honey or malt. Products labelled in this way must carry full nutritional labelling.

Unsweetened means that the food does not contain any of the above sugars nor does it contain artificial sweeteners or sorbitol or mannitol, which are substances related to sugars.

Low-joule is a term restricted to a small number of foods, such as low-joule soft drinks. The foods must contain no more than 70 kJ per reference quantity, which in the case of soft drink is 200 mL.

It is illegal for food labels to refer to any disease or physiological condition – for example, a food cannot be labelled 'diabetic' or 'slimming'.

SUGAR CONTENT OF FOODS

Food	Average serving	Sugar (g per serve)
Fruit gums	3-4 (10 g)	4
Boiled lollies	2 (10 g)	9
Peppermints	3 (10 g)	10
Caramels	2 (10 g)	7
Liquorice allsorts	3 (10 g)	7
Milk chocolate	4 squares from block (24 g)	14
Health food bar	1 (40 g)	9
Ice cream	1 large scoop (50 g)	10
Water ice block	1 (80 g)	14
Chocolate-coated ice cream	1 (70 g)	19
Soft drink	1 can 370 mL	37
Flavoured milk drink	1 carton 300 mL	27
Cordial diluted 1:4	1 glass 250 mL	18
Jam	1 tablespoon (20 g)	14
Pre-sweetened cereal	average bowl 30 g	2-15

* Figures are for total sugars present in the food, which includes naturally occurring sugars (fructose, glucose, lactose) as well as sucrose derived from added cane sugar. Sucrose, however, is the predominant sugar.

Weight Check

Your weight – your health. Health promoters and the media may have you confused about what is the right weight for you.

Too much or too little weight can affect the way our bodies function and the way we feel about ourselves, our food and eating. There is no such thing as a single ideal weight for any height, but there is a healthy weight range which is based on a Body Mass Index (BMI) of 20 to 25.

The BMI is a measure of body fat in adults. Studies over a long period have shown that people in this weight range are less likely to suffer from illness or die prematurely. Moving outside the range, in either direction, increases the risk.

> You can work out your BMI by dividing your weight in kilograms by the square of your height in metres.
>
> $$\text{BMI} = \frac{\text{Weight (kg)}}{\text{Height (m)} \times \text{Height (m)}}$$

Overweight people have a higher incidence of high blood pressure, high blood fats and more heart disease, diabetes, gout and gall bladder disease compared with the general population. Apart from the risk of physical ill health, knowing that you are overweight can affect your confidence in yourself, reducing your self-esteem and making you less willing and less able to be active and outgoing. On the other hand, knowing that you are able to maintain your weight at a healthy level adds to your confidence and feeling of well-being.

WEIGHT GAIN

It is true that 'fatness runs in families', but if your parents are overweight don't despair, just take it as a warning that you are one of the people who most needs to practise prevention. Weight can only be gained when the kilojoules (calories) provided by the food consumed exceed the kilojoules used by the body. When people combine their high-kilojoule intake with a low-kilojoule output the excess kilojoules are stored as body fat. An excess of 32 000 kilojoules is stored as approximately one kilogram of fat.

The Cause

△ Food is so attractive and tempting and we have an abundant supply all-year-round.

△ The level of interest in food and eating has been stimulated by comparative affluence, travel and the diversity of foods available.

△ Entertainment and hospitality more than ever centre around food.

△ 'Grazing' has become a way of life for many. They often snack on foods loaded with fat and/or sugar.

△ Boredom – it's so easy to fill empty time by eating. People don't always eat because they are hungry.

△ Alcohol is a significant source of kilojoules (calories) for some people – each gram provides 29 kilojoules.

△ Too little physical activity.

> ### WEIGHTY MATTERS
> Although some authorities say that our weight should remain the same throughout our adult years, both women and men tend to gain weight after their 30s. The average person gains 3 kg (half a stone) between his or her 25th and 35th birthday, but a small percentage put on much more than this (which raises blood pressure and cholesterol levels). But once past the age of 55 the kilos usually start to drop off, with women losing more than men.

EARLY WARNING SIGNS

☐ Be honest – are you puffing up the stairs?

☐ Are you choosing looser clothes?

☐ Have you let out your belt notch?

Do something now – it will be easier now than later.

YOUR ACTION PLAN TO PREVENT WEIGHT GAIN OR LOSE WEIGHT

1 Set realistic short-term and long-term goals for weight loss.

2 Follow the Healthy Diet Pyramid plan.

3 Keep all meals and snacks low in fat and sugar.

4 Eat lots of vegetables and fruit.

5 If you drink alcohol, be moderate – have only one or two drinks two or three times a week.

6 Whatever your age, include some enjoyable daily exercise.

7 Drink more water.

> ### AVERAGE ALCOHOL CONTENT OF BEER AND WINE (g)
>
> | | | |
> |---|---|---|
> | Standard beer | 1 can (375 mL) | 16 g |
> | 'Light' beer | 1 can (375 mL) | 10 g |
> | Dry wine | 1 glass (115 mL) | 12 g |

Healthy Weight Range Chart

These healthy weight ranges are based on data from a number of studies which show acceptable weights consistent with lowest mortality.

FOR WOMEN AND MEN 18 YEARS UPWARDS		
Height (without shoes)		**Body Weight** (in light clothing without shoes)
140 cm	4 ft 7 ins	39 - 49 kg
142	4 8	40 - 50
144	4 9	41 - 52
146	4 $9^{1}/_{2}$	43 - 53
148	4 10	44 - 56
150	4 11	45 - 56
152	5 0	46 - 58
154	5 1	47 - 59
156	5 $1^{1}/_{2}$	49 - 61
158	5 2	50 - 62
160	5 3	51 - 64
162	5 4	52 - 66
164	5 $4^{1}/_{2}$	54 - 67
166	5 5	55 - 69
168	5 6	56 - 71
170	5 7	58 - 72
172	5 8	59 - 74
174	5 $8^{1}/_{2}$	61 - 76
176	5 9	62 - 77
178	5 10	63 - 79
180	5 11	65 - 81
182	6 0	66 - 83
184	6 $^{1}/_{2}$	68 - 85
186	6 1	69 - 86
188	6 2	71 - 88
190	6 3	72 - 90
192	6 4	74 - 92
194	6 $4^{1}/_{2}$	75 - 94
196	6 5	77 - 96
198	6 6	78 - 98
200	6 7	80 - 100

METRIC WEIGHT CONVERTER		
kg	**st**	**lb**
1.0		2 lb
6.4	1 st	
10	1 st	8 lb
20	3 st	2 lb
40	6 st	4 lb
44	6 st	13 lb
46	7 st	4 lb
48	7 st	8 lb
50	7 st	13 lb
52	8 st	3 lb
54	8 st	7 lb
56	8 st	12 lb
58	9 st	2 lb
60	9 st	6 lb
62	9 st	11 lb
64	10 st	2 lb
66	10 st	6 lb
68	10 st	10 lb
70	11 st	1 lb
72	11 st	5 lb
74	11 st	10 lb
76	12 st	
78	12 st	4 lb
80	12 st	9 lb
82	12 st	13 lb
84	13 st	4 lb
86	13 st	8 lb
88	13 st	13 lb
89	14 st	
91	14 st	4 lb
94	14 st	11 lb
99	15 st	8 lb
127	20 st	

Your Child's Weight

THE OVERWEIGHT CHILD

The best help that Mum and Dad can give is to set a good example. Having overweight parents increases a child's risk of becoming overweight. Set realistic short-term and long-term goals.

△ Encourage children to enjoy meals that emphasise fruits and vegetables, wholegrain cereals and bread.

△ Keep meals low in fat by using lean meat, removing the skin from the chicken, using reduced-fat or low-fat milk, yoghurt and cheese and just a scraping of butter or polyunsaturated margarine on bread.

△ Reduce the use of fried and crumbed foods.

△ Avoid fatty snack foods like potato crisps and use low-fat snacks like fruit, vegetable pieces and low-fat yoghurt.

Overweight children are usually great television watchers. This means that they are inactive and vulnerable to advertising which often promotes high-fat and/or sugar snack foods. Pressures from their friends may also encourage them to want these foods. Don't expect the child to give up snacks altogether. Encourage their occasional use and offer enjoyable alternatives. In other words, establish healthy habits!

Exercise is very important. Overweight children are often underactive and reluctant to take part in sport because of their poor performance. Encourage non-competitive outdoor activities like cycling, walking, running in the park and swimming. It's better still if the rest of the family join in!

THE UNDERWEIGHT CHILD

Heredity influences the tendency to become underweight as well as overweight. A child may be skinny because that is his or her inherited body build or because he or she does not eat enough. There are several possible causes.

△ The child is too busy with other activities.

△ Family discord creates a poor atmosphere at mealtimes.

△ Too much food is served at family meals or the food is too highly spiced.

△ The child's likes and dislikes are not given sufficient attention.

△ The child eats lollies and fatty snacks between meals.

△ The child misses meals like breakfast through lack of time.

△ The child is too tired to eat. This can sometimes be caused by too much television and not enough sleep.

What can you do?

△ Arrange for a full medical check-up.

△ Set a good example and create a happy mealtime atmosphere.

△ Provide smaller meals and healthy, more substantial between-meal snacks.

△ Plan meals, including nourishing snacks.

△ Plan activities around food – picnics, barbecues, parties, food shopping and cooking.

△ Don't force and badger at mealtimes – relax and enjoy!

FIGHTING FAT

Stick to the following guidelines to ensure your children do not become overweight.

▲ Try not to offer food as a reward for good behaviour. A major problem is food featured on television. Children see soft drinks, sweets, lollies, heavily sugared cereals, ice creams and salted snacks and demand them.

▲ Set a good example and keep less healthy food to a minimum.

▲ Encourage exercise and outdoor play.

▲ When children are sick, we tend to pamper them with treats. Be aware of this when they return to better health.

▲ Insecurity and emotional problems are often causes of overeating. Perceived rejection from parents, rivalry, moving to a new neighbourhood or school, feeling left out or unhappy are all triggers.

▲ Ban thoughtless snacking in front of television.

▲ Explain your attitude to family and friends. It's tempting for them to hand out sweets at visits, but this is unhealthy in the long term.

MENU OUTLINE FOR SCHOOL-AGED CHILD

Breakfast	See breakfast section for hot ideas Fresh, canned or frozen fruit or fruit juice Wholegrain cereal – porridge or ready-to-eat packet cereal Wholegrain or mixed grain toast Scraping polyunsaturated margarine, reduced-fat spread or butter Honey, jam or peanut butter Low-fat or reduced fat milk
Lunch	Include bread and salad vegetables with lean meat, chicken without the skin, fresh and canned fish, baked beans and other legumes or cheese – including reduced- and low-fat varieties Fresh, canned or stewed fruit Plain or flavoured milk, fruit juice or water
Dinner	Choose from lean meat or chicken, fish or vegetarian recipes in our What's for Dinner section Serve lots of potato, pasta or rice and fresh, frozen or canned vegetables To finish the meal see our Delicious Desserts section or serve fresh, stewed or canned fruit with low-fat yoghurt, ice cream or milk ice confections, rice or custard with fruit and reduced- or low-fat milk For hungry children serve bread with dinner

Fad Diets

There are no magic ways to shed weight. Don't be fooled by wonder diets, pills, formulae, herbal extracts, creams and exercise machines promising quick weight loss.

FAD DIETS DON'T WORK

If it took you several months to put on those extra kilograms, expect it to take a similar time to get it off.

You will lose weight on a fad diet in the short term but what you'll lose is water and lean muscle, not fat. 'Crash' diets, high in protein and fat, lack carbohydrate, and the muscle quickly uses up its glycogen stores first for energy. Every gram of glycogen contains 3 grams of water, so the loss of 600 grams of muscle glycogen in the average person results in about a 1.5-2 kg (3-5 lb) weight loss. When glycogen stores are depleted, the body starts breaking down protein or lean muscle tissue to glucose. You don't want to lose lean muscle, as this keeps you trim and taut and helps you burn kilojoules (calories) fast. Fat will be burned slowly so expect to lose only 0.5-1 kg each week.

Fad or crash diets can be boring, usually involve a limited number of foods, don't fit in with family meals and certainly play havoc with your social life. You'll feel deprived and the temptation to break out will strengthen.

Fad diets are often nutritionally unbalanced, being deficient in carbohydrates, dietary fibre, vitamins and minerals, as well as kilojoules (calories).

Once you've lost weight you must keep it off. Ideally, a diet should teach you a better way of eating – a return to your previous eating habits results in a see-saw pattern of weight loss and gain. This is damaging for both your health and your self esteem.

DANGERS OF FAD DIETS

Because fad diets are often nutritionally unsound they should not be followed.

Low-carbohydrate diets can result in ketosis (an accumulation of fatty substances in the blood) and cause side-effects such as dizziness, dehydration, high cholesterol levels, constipation and kidney problems.

Deaths from heart failure have occurred due to the abuse of high-protein supplements (liquid or powder). These products are composed of protein and protein hydrolysates and lack other essential nutrients.

Fasting without medical supervision is dangerous and usually results in a general feeling of being unwell.

10 foolproof tips for better eating

1 Chew slowly. Eating slowly allows more time for your stomach to signal the brain when full.

2 Sit down to eat. Make yourself sit down, this helps you to concentrate on and enjoy every kilojoule.

3 Keep food out of sight. Store high-temptation food in containers, in cupboards or at the back of the fridge. Often the mere sight of food triggers off hunger attacks (not true hunger).

4 Use a small plate. Serving food on a smaller plate, a simple eye trick, makes a small serve look generous.

5 Concentrate while eating. Do NOT read, watch television, write or talk on the phone when you eat or you are likely to eat too much.

6 Don't have two competing pressures. Don't start a diet when you are trying to break another habit or when a big decision is imminent.

7 Don't skip meals. Strange as it sounds, this often leads to consuming more kilojoules, not less!

8 Remove leftovers straight away. Clear the table after each meal and dispose of leftovers. Don't give yourself the opportunity to pick at uneaten food. Don't nibble at your children's leftover food.

9 Keep busy. The busier you are, the less time you'll have to be tempted to overeat.

10 Stop negative thinking. Don't feel sorry for yourself. Enjoy your better health and think about one day at a time.

From Slim to Thin

Today's fashion industry has focused on slimness as an ideal. But there is a point at which 'slim' becomes dangerously thin.

Standards of female beauty have varied through the ages and in different cultures. In the past, artists depicted women with heavier, rounder, fuller figures – rounded bosoms, bottoms and curves were considered beautiful. An indication that attitudes were changing came in the 1920s with the flappers bandaging their breasts to achieve a flat, slim look. Since the Second World War, the slim ideal has again become fashionable. Unfortunately, slim has come to mean thin. Thinness has been promoted as equalling beauty, success, happiness and self-worth.

The thin standard has been taken over and vigorously pushed by television advertising, women's magazines, newspapers and films.

Women's magazines publish an endless stream of diets – some nutritionally unsound. Many normal-weight or even underweight women and young girls, confused by the pressures, are worried because they incorrectly see themselves as fat. When the fashion industry has to use younger and younger models with immature and childlike figures to meet society's illusions about beauty and body shape, the thinness ideal is clearly irrational and dangerous.

△ Thinness is not necessary for good health.

△ Being 'underweight' carries its own health risks.

△ Extreme dieting can distort body image, cause hormone imbalances, hasten the ageing process and destroy health.

NEW DIET CHECK LIST

Does the diet:

△ Make extravagant claims about enabling you to lose weight quickly and effortlessly?

△ Include very high-fat foods with little carbohydrate and fibre foods?

△ Have limited choice of foods?

△ Use exercise machines, rather than encouraging you to exercise?

△ Require you to buy special diet supplements or pills and potions?

△ Allow you to eat as much as you like of any one food and not put on weight?

△ Highlight the particular importance of one food in the diet, giving it 'miracle' properties?

△ Emphasise the importance of combining foods, that is, one food should not be eaten with another?

△ Are the promoters selling an expensive supplement or an 'aid' to dieting?

If the answer to any of these questions is YES, then this is not a sound diet. Give it a miss!

ANOREXIA NERVOSA

In Australia, where 43 per cent of women are overweight or obese and many girls are overweight, it is a paradox that anorexia nervosa has become a serious problem.

Anorexia nervosa is reported to be increasing in a number of countries. In Australia one in 100 teenage girls will at some time suffer from anorexia nervosa. The preoccupation of young girls with fad slimming diets encourages disturbed eating behaviour and increases the risk of anorexia nervosa.

Anorexia nervosa is self-starvation. The sufferer, usually a teenage girl or young woman, is terrified of gaining weight and getting fat. Although below the healthy weight range they see themselves as overweight. It is a serious, life-threatening disease and early diagnosis and treatment is critical.

6 important points to remember when looking for the ideal diet for you

1 It must be nutritionally balanced, with a variety of nutritious foods like breads and cereals, fruit and vegetables, lean meat and dairy products and with limited quantities of polyunsaturated margarine, oils or butter.

2 It must be flexible and varied to fit in with your lifestyle and family.

3 It can be followed for long periods of time, unlike most crash diets.

4 It must be moderate in energy – between 4000 to 6000 kilojoules (1000 to 1500 Calories) a day.

5 It must allow a modest weight loss of 0.5 to 1 kg per week – this is fat, not water loss.

6 It uses ordinary foods and does not require special diet foods exclusively.

Understanding Food Labels

Food labels can provide a wealth of useful information about the food we eat. Four out of five people usually read the label of a raw or unfamiliar food before buying it. They are looking for nutritional rather than practical information, such as the contents in general, the presence of additives, and the sugar or salt content.

KILOJOULES VS CALORIES

Kilojoules are the metric units of energy, which are gradually replacing calories on food labels and diets. If you wish to calculate the number of calories from kilojoules, divide the kilojoules by 4.186 or simply by 4.2. Thus the recommended weight-loss diet for women should be no less than 5000 kilojoules a day, which is equivalent to 1200 Calories. Technically speaking, the word 'Calories' (written with a capital C when preceded by a figure) is an abbreviation for 'kilocalories', where the capital C stands for the 'kilo'.

WHAT'S IN THE PACK?

All packaged food should include the following information:

△ The prescribed name or appropriate designation of the food.

△ The name and business address of the manufacturer, the packer or vendor and, in the case of imported food, the name and address of the importer.

△ The country of origin of the food.

△ Some form of identification of the premises where the food was produced and the production lot involved (important in cases of recall or contamination).

△ A list of ingredients.

△ A Use- or Sell-by date or date of packaging.

Ingredients

All ingredients must be listed in descending order of proportion by weight, except that water may be declared at the end simply as 'WATER ADDED'.

By checking the first three ingredients on the list, you will know the three major ingredients in the food.

For example, most biscuits will have FLOUR, SUGAR and some type of FAT/OIL as their major components, which appear at the beginning of the list.

Cheese, alcoholic beverages and very small food packages are not required to carry an ingredients list. However, if you have any queries about the product's contents, you can write direct to the manufacturer.

WHOLEMEAL BREAD

A typical nutrition information panel for a loaf of wholemeal bread is shown in the accompanying table. It states the nutrient content of the bread in terms of its standard serving size (here, one slice) and per 100 grams, which is equivalent to approximately 4 slices. Note that the fat listed is total fat and does not distinguish between saturated or unsaturated types, the food must have twice as much polyunsaturated as saturated fatty acids. The carbohydrate is divided into two types: total carbohydrate (available carbohydrate excluding dietary fibre), which comprises the starchy carbohydrates; plus sugars. Sugars are listed separately, which is helpful for those people wanting to reduce their sugar intake. To work out the amount of starch present, simply subtract the figure for sugars from that of the total.

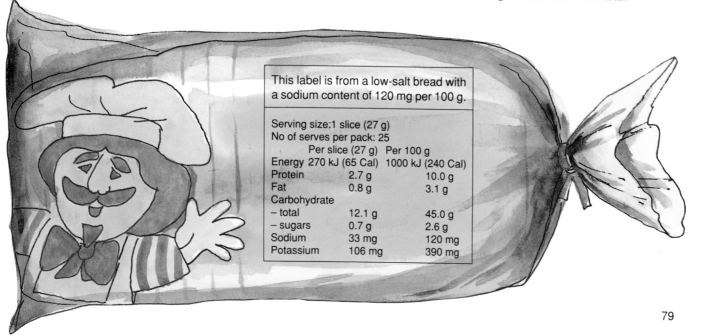

This label is from a low-salt bread with a sodium content of 120 mg per 100 g.

	Per slice (27 g)	Per 100 g
Serving size: 1 slice (27 g)		
No of serves per pack: 25		
Energy	270 kJ (65 Cal)	1000 kJ (240 Cal)
Protein	2.7 g	10.0 g
Fat	0.8 g	3.1 g
Carbohydrate		
– total	12.1 g	45.0 g
– sugars	0.7 g	2.6 g
Sodium	33 mg	120 mg
Potassium	106 mg	390 mg

Food Additives

Additives must be shown with other ingredients by their functional class name followed immediately by their full chemical name or a number. For example, a label may tell you that preservative sodium metabisulphite is present by stating PRESERVATIVE (SODIUM METABISULPHITE) or simply list PRESERVATIVE (223). Anyone sensitive to sulphites would then know it was present and could avoid that particular product.

The number system has been operating in Europe for many years. Imported foods at the supermarket have numbers with the prefix 'E'. These numbers correspond to the Australian system, making it easy and universal. Adverse effects of food additives on health (believed to affect about 5 per cent of the population) have received a good deal of publicity in recent years. The most common reactions are recurrent hives, headaches, stomach upsets, bowel disturbances and behavioural changes such as hyperactivity. Problems with a true allergic basis such as asthma and eczema can also be aggravated by food components.

ADDITIVES AND HEALTH

People who are upset by additives usually react to naturally occurring food chemicals as well. The most important of these are salicylates (or natural aspirins), a group of substances widespread in fruit, vegetables, spices, herbs (particularly mint), tea, coffee and wine.

Natural benzoates from berry fruits, tea, pepper, honey and vegetables also trigger reactions – as do benzoates added as preserving agents to certain commercial foods.

Simply banning food additives will not help overcome allergies. The body does not distinguish between 'natural' or 'synthetic' and so all sources of these substances must be avoided or limited.

Skin prick and blood tests are not considered reliable for identifying the problem chemicals in food. Professional advice from a specialist or

---

APPROVED ADDITIVE CLASS NAMES AND THEIR ROLE AND FUNCTIONS

△ *Anti-caking agents* prevent powdered products such as icing sugar and powdered milk from sticking together and becoming lumpy.

△ *Antioxidants* stop oils and fats from turning rancid and other food from discolouring.

△ *Artificial colours* restore colour lost during processing and make food look more appealing.

△ *Emulsifiers* prevent mixtures of oil and water from separating out.

△ *Flavours* produce uniform flavouring and restore flavours lost during processing.

△ *Flavour enhancers* do not add flavour themselves, but intensify the flavour of existing ingredients.

△ *Food acids* produce a consistent acidity in foods and give a flavour balance between acidity and sweetness.

△ *Humectants* maintain moisture and prevent food from drying out.

△ *Preservatives* slow the growth of undesirable moulds and bacteria and extend the shelf-life of foods.

△ *Thickeners* improve the texture and consistency of foods.

△ *Vegetable gums* thicken and stabilise foods.

Note: Remember that all additives undergo rigorous review before approval and are only permitted in foods for which they are specifically approved and only up to a maximum dosage. A full list of additives and their code numbers is available as a pamphlet 'Identifying Food Additives' from the Commonwealth Department of Community Services and Health in Canberra or the Australian Nutrition Foundation in your state. British readers can obtain a full list of permitted additives from H. M. Stationary office in London.

---

the allergy clinic of a large hospital is the only answer. A strict exclusion or elimination diet, based on a limited number of foods, is usually prescribed for a fixed period (say 2-3 weeks) followed by a systematic trial-and-error set of challenges. A challenge is a known dose of a suspected compound such as purified salicylates, yeast, amines, benzoates, glutamates, artificial colours.

Once problem chemicals are identified, proper food labelling makes shopping easier and safer for allergy-prone people.

Sulphites and Asthma

One group of preservatives, sulphites, are now known to be a danger to some asthmatics, triggering moderate to severe asthma attacks, even death, in sulphite-sensitive people. For most people, however, sulphites are a safe group of additives. They are, in fact, very useful preserving agents, preventing spoilage and discolouration

in a wide range of foods.

Sulphur has been used since ancient times to preserve wine and is still important today as an antioxidant in the wine industry – it is listed on the label of wines as PRESERVATIVE (220).

Foods permitted to contain sulphites are pickled onions and other pickled vegetables, sausages and sausage mince, some drinks, dried tree fruit (dried apricots, apples and pears).

Asthmatics who wish to avoid sulphites should look for the additive numbers 220, 221, 222, 223 and 224 on food packs.

Artificial Colours

Artificial colours are another group of additives which have come under a great deal of attack. They generally appear in foods aimed at youngsters, such as soft drinks, cordial, ice blocks and lollies, but are also used to add colour to packet cake mixes, dessert toppings, biscuits and jelly crystals. Obviously eye appeal is very important today in the selling of food, and colour plays a key role in consumer expectation of food quality. Colouring agents are largely cosmetic with no other technical function.

Monosodium Glutamate (MSG)

MSG is the sodium salt of glutamic acid. It is a widely used flavour enhancer both in restaurant dishes and in packaged foods. It intensifies the flavour of savoury foods, particularly protein foods like meat and fish, and is often present in packet soups, stock cubes, noodle mixes and sauces.

Research has shown that MSG eaten in moderate amounts causes no harm. However, it can trigger asthma attacks in sensitive people and can produce nausea, headache, palpitations and chest tightening after a meal. Although uncomfortable, the symptoms are short-lived and leave no after-effects.

MSG also occurs quite naturally in many common foods. Tomatoes, mushrooms and cheese contain significant amounts, and this accounts for their ability to add a rich flavour in cooking.

A recent Australian study (NSW Health Department) found that restaurants are using MSG in a balanced and proper manner; many restaurants now also advertise that no MSG is used in cooking.

Anyone wishing to avoid MSG should check with the restaurant when making a booking. In packaged foods, MSG is indicated on the label by the words FLAVOUR ENHANCER (621).

NUTRITION LABELLING

More and more food packs today provide detailed nutrition information for consumers. Nutrition labelling is compulsory when a nutrition 'claim' is made on the pack, suggesting or implying that the food has a nutritional benefit such as being high in fibre or cholesterol-free.

A special nutrition information panel is shown on the pack detailing the kilojoule (calorie) content of the food and its protein, fat, total carbohydrate, sugars, sodium and potassium contents per serving and per 100 grams (or per 100 mL in the case of liquids). This enables consumers to check and compare the nutritional value of different foods.

For example, if you are trying to reduce your intake of fat, you can see at a glance which foods have less than 5 grams of fat per 100 grams (or 5 per cent) which means they have very little fat indeed.

In another instance, if you were counting kilojoules, a quick check of a food pack can tell you exactly how many are contained in a serving of snack food or a beverage and you can compare this to your total daily allowance of, say, 5000 kilojoules (1200 Calories).

ADDITIVES MOST LIKELY TO CAUSE ADVERSE REACTIONS IN SENSITIVE PEOPLE

Artificial colours:		Preservatives:	
Tartrazine	102	Sulphites	220, 221, 222, 223, 224
Yellow 2G	107	Benzoates	210, 211, 212, 213
Sunset yellow FCF	110	Sorbates	200, 201, 202, 203
Cochineal	120	**Mineral salts:**	
Carmoisine	122	Nitrites	249, 250
Amaranth	123	Nitrates	251, 252
Ponceau 4R	124	**Others:**	
Erythrosine	127	Glutamates	621, 622, 623
Indigo carmine	132	(including MSG)	
Brilliant blue FCF	133	Gallates	310, 311, 312
Caramel	150	Butylated	
Brilliant black BN	151	hydroxyanisole (BHA) 320	
Brown HT	155	Butylated	
		hydroxytoluene (BHT) 321	

Note: Certain natural food components can also cause adverse reactions.

Picnics and Barbecues

Picnics and barbecues are a great source of family pleasure and provide time to relax in an attractive outdoor setting. Apart from their fun aspect, outdoor meals present an excellent opportunity for eating raw vegetables in the form of salads (coleslaw, Waldorf and mixed greens) and as an accompaniment to dips like avocado, hummus, cucumber and yoghurt.

❖

GREEN BEAN AND WALNUT SALAD

The secret of a good mixed salad is to achieve a contrast of colours, textures and flavours. For example, the combination of avocado, cooked beans and walnuts or perhaps lettuce, tomato and grated carrot. The addition of corn or cherry tomatoes to a green salad is always eye catching. All leafy ingredients should be well dried so that only a minimum of dressing is needed.

Serves 8

- ☐ **410 g (13 oz) green beans, trimmed**
- ☐ **6 tomatoes, quartered**
- ☐ **2 sticks celery, finely sliced**
- ☐ **1 carrot, grated**
- ☐ **lettuce leaves or raddichio leaves, washed and dried**
- ☐ **1 apple, quartered, cored and sliced**
- ☐ **2 tablespoons chopped walnuts**

DRESSING
- ☐ **1 small clove garlic, chopped**
- ☐ **2 teaspoons red wine vinegar**
- ☐ **1$^1/_2$ tablespoons olive oil**
- ☐ **freshly ground black pepper**

1   Steam or microwave beans until just tender. Refresh under cold running water and drain.
2   Combine beans, tomatoes, celery, carrot, lettuce, apple and walnuts in a salad bowl. Refrigerate until ready to serve.
3   To make dressing, place garlic, vinegar, oil and pepper in a screwtop jar. Shake well to combine. Just prior to serving, pour dressing over salad and gently toss to coat ingredients.

350 kilojoules (85 Calories) per serve

Fat	5.5 g	high
Cholesterol	none	
Fibre	3.8 g	medium
Sodium	30 mg	low

❖

BARBECUED LAMB AND VEGETABLE KEBABS

Kebabs can be easily made with all types of lean meat. You can vary the seasoning using different spices, herbs, lemon juice or low-salt sauces to suit your family's tastes.

Serves 4

- ☐ **500 g (1 lb) lean boneless lamb, trimmed of all visible fat and cut into 2.5 cm (1 in) cubes**
- ☐ **1 teaspoon polyunsaturated oil**
- ☐ **$^1/_4$ teaspoon ground cumin**
- ☐ **freshly ground black pepper**
- ☐ **$^1/_2$ teaspoon chopped fresh lemon thyme**
- ☐ **16 button mushrooms**
- ☐ **1 green capsicum, cut into 2.5 cm (1 in) cubes**
- ☐ **16 cherry tomatoes**

1   Place lamb, oil, cumin, pepper and lemon thyme in a bowl and mix well to coat lamb. Refrigerate for 2-3 hours or overnight if possible.
2   Thread lamb, mushrooms, capsicum, and tomatoes alternately onto oiled wooden skewers. Refrigerate if not using immediately.
3   Cook kebabs on a hot barbecue for 5 minutes each side or until meat is cooked to your liking.

800 kilojoules (195 Calories) per serve

Fat	6 g	medium
Cholesterol	83 mg	medium
Fibre	2.6 g	medium
Sodium	105 mg	low

Green Bean and Walnut Salad, Barbecued Lamb and Vegetable Kebabs, Two Potato Salads in One,

TWO POTATO SALADS IN ONE

Most people love potato salad, but young children often prefer it without the herbs, onion and other flavourings that adults love. So before adding those special extras to your potato salad, keep a little aside for less sophisticated palates and everyone will be happy.

Serves 4

- [ ] **12 baby new potatoes**
- [ ] **1/2 red capsicum, diced**
- [ ] **1 small white onion, finely chopped**
- [ ] **1 tablespoon chopped fresh chives**
- [ ] **1 tablespoon chopped fresh basil**

DRESSING
- [ ] **1 teaspoon red wine vinegar**
- [ ] **1 tablespoon light olive oil**
- [ ] **freshly ground black pepper**

1   Steam, microwave or boil potatoes in their jackets until just tender.

2   Peel potatoes, cut in half and set half aside. Place remaining potatoes in a bowl. Add capsicum, onion and chives, toss lightly, to combine.

3   To make dressing, place vinegar, oil and pepper in a screwtop jar. Shake well to combine. Pour half the dressing over the potato salad and the remainder over the potato halves to make the children's salad.

560 kilojoules (135 Calories) per serve

Fat	5 g	medium
Cholesterol	none	
Fibre	4.4 g	medium
Sodium	50 mg	low

BARBECUE TIPS

▲ If using a hotplate to barbecue, heat well before placing the meat on it. When cooking is completed, scrape off any residue so it's clean for the next use. Some barbecue chefs like to clean the hotplate with a glass of wine.

▲ When barbecuing always have a bottle of water with a sprinkle top on hand so that you can douse any flames that are caused by fat dripping on to the coals.

SPICY PICNIC CHICKEN AND VEGETABLES

A lovely picnic dish that can be prepared the day before it is required. The final flavour is aromatic rather than hot. Potato or rice salad is the ideal accompaniment.

Serves 4

- ☐ **1 teaspoon olive oil**
- ☐ **1 teaspoon grated fresh ginger**
- ☐ **1 small onion, chopped**
- ☐ **1 clove garlic, crushed**
- ☐ **1 teaspoon mild curry powder**
- ☐ **4 chicken pieces, trimmed of all visible fat and skin removed**
- ☐ **4 tomatoes, peeled and diced**
- ☐ **2 zucchini, diced**
- ☐ **1 cup (250 mL/8 fl.oz) chicken stock, no-added-salt**
- ☐ **freshly ground black pepper**
- ☐ **1¹/₂ cups (185 g/6 oz) shelled peas**

1   Heat oil in a large saucepan and cook ginger, onion and garlic for 2 minutes. Stir in curry powder, add chicken pieces and stir well to coat with curry mixture.

2   Add tomatoes, zucchini and stock, season to taste with pepper. Cover and simmer for 15 minutes.

3   Fold through peas and cook for 10 minutes longer or until chicken is cooked. Transfer chicken mixture to a dish, allow to cool then refrigerate to chill. A light gel forms when the dish has been chilled.

930 kilojoules (190 Calories) per serve

Fat	7 g	medium
Cholesterol	85 mg	medium
Fibre	2.8 g	medium
Sodium	155 mg	low

❖

SURPRISE FISH PARCELS

Fish cooked in foil is excellent barbecue fare and a good alternative to red meat. The choices of seasonings are endless – tomatoes, lemon, orange slices, mushrooms, zucchini, herbs and spices to name a few.

Serves 4

- ☐ **2 tomatoes, thinly sliced**
- ☐ **8 basil leaves**
- ☐ **500 g (1 lb) fish fillets**
- ☐ **1 teaspoon olive oil**
- ☐ **1 tablespoon lemon juice**
- ☐ **freshly ground black pepper**

1   Cut four pieces of aluminium foil about 30 cm (12 in) long. Place 2 tomato slices and 2 basil leaves in the centre of each piece of foil. Divide fish between parcels and top with remaining tomato.

3   Combine oil, lemon juice and pepper. Pour over fish and seal foil parcels. Cook on a hot barbecue for 5-10 minutes or until fish flakes when tested with a fork. Serve immediately.

570 kilojoules (135 Calories) per serve

Fat	4 g	medium
Cholesterol	75 mg	medium
Fibre	0.9 g	low
Sodium	150 mg	low

Below: Spicy Picnic Chicken and Vegetables
Right: Family Hamburgers, Pineapple Coleslaw

PINEAPPLE COLESLAW

This is a great classic salad, the vitamin and fibre-rich cabbage and carrot are thought to play an important role in preventing cancer. The yoghurt dressing makes a light, interesting alternative to the heavier mayonnaise so often used.

Serves 6

- ☐ ¹/₂ **small cabbage, finely shredded**
- ☐ **1 carrot, grated**
- ☐ **1 small onion, finely chopped (optional)**
- ☐ **1 tablespoon sultanas**
- ☐ **2 slices pineapple, in natural juice, drained and chopped**
- ☐ **2 tablespoons low-fat unflavoured yoghurt**
- ☐ **juice of ¹/₂ lemon**
- ☐ **freshly ground black pepper**

Place cabbage, carrot, onion, sultanas, pineapple, yoghurt and lemon juice in a salad bowl. Toss lightly to combine and season to taste with pepper, then refrigerate until ready to serve.

180 kilojoules (45 Calories) per serve		
Fat	negligible	
Cholesterol	negligible	
Fibre	3.0 g	medium
Sodium	25 mg	low

❖

FAMILY HAMBURGERS

Mincing your own meat will ensure that you have the leanest possible mince.

Serves 6

- ☐ **500 g (1 lb) lean minced meat**
- ☐ **3 tablespoons cold water**
- ☐ **1 tablespoon chopped onion**
- ☐ **2 tablespoons chopped fresh parsley**
- ☐ **freshly ground black pepper**
- ☐ **1 tomato, thinly sliced**
- ☐ **1 small carrot, grated**
- ☐ **6 shredded lettuce leaves**
- ☐ **6 wholegrain rolls, split and toasted**

1   Place minced meat, cold water, onion, parsley and pepper to taste, in a bowl. Mix well to combine all ingredients.

2   Divide meat mixture into six portions and form into patties. Refrigerate if not using immediately. Cook hamburgers on a hot barbecue for 3-4 minutes each side. Avoid overcooking as the meat will become dry.

3   Place tomato, carrot and lettuce on bottom half of roll, top with meat pattie and replace the top of the roll.

1630 kilojoules (390 Calories) per serve		
Fat	7.5 g	low
Cholesterol	75 mg	medium
Fibre	8.4 g	high
Sodium	580 mg	medium

B A R B E C U E   T I P

▲   Don't slash steak to see if it is cooked, instead press gently with blunt tongs. Rare steak is springy to touch, slightly springy when medium and firm when well done.

SALAD IN A LOAF

We have made a curried chicken salad to go in our loaf, but you might prefer to have just a plain chicken, a meat, tuna or salmon salad, according to the occasion and the tastes of those you are feeding. This is a wonderful picnic dish as it can be made the day before the picnic and wrapped in foil. It keeps happily in the refrigerator.

Serves 6
- [ ] **1 rectangular loaf wholemeal bread**
- [ ] **lettuce leaves**

CHICKEN SALAD
- [ ] **1 large cold cooked chicken**
- [ ] **2 teaspoons polyunsaturated oil**
- [ ] **1 onion, chopped**
- [ ] **1 clove garlic, crushed**
- [ ] **1 teaspoon finely chopped fresh ginger**
- [ ] **1 stick celery, chopped**
- [ ] **1 small red capsicum, chopped**
- [ ] **2 teaspoons curry powder**
- [ ] **1 tablespoon tomato relish**
- [ ] **1 tablespoon mango or fruit chutney**
- [ ] **2 tablespoons mayonnaise**
- [ ] **3 tablespoons low-fat unflavoured yoghurt**
- [ ] **freshly ground black pepper**

1   To make chicken salad, remove skin from chicken and discard. Remove flesh from the chicken and cut in cubes. Heat oil in a non-stick frypan and cook onion, garlic and ginger, gently for 5 minutes. Add celery, capsicum and curry powder and cook for 5 minutes longer. Remove pan from heat and mix in relish and chutney. Set aside and allow to cool.
2   Combine mayonnaise and yoghurt in a bowl, stir in vegetable mixture and chicken. Season to taste with pepper.
3   Cut the top off the loaf and scoop out the middle so that only the crust remains to make a large bread case. Reserve top of loaf, the crumbs from the centre will not be used in this recipe, but can be made into breadcrumbs. Line bread case with lettuce leaves and fill with chicken salad. Top with remaining lettuce leaves and top of loaf. Wrap filled loaf in foil and refrigerate until ready to take on your picnic. To serve, unwrap and cut into thick slices.

1460 kilojoules (345 Calories) per serve

Fat	14 g	medium
Cholesterol	153 mg	high
Fibre	3.0 g	medium
Sodium	430 mg	medium

DRIED FRUIT MEDLEY

A tasty combination of dried fruit which can be made up the day before a picnic and refrigerated. You might like to use a herb tea for the marinade in this recipe.

Serves 6
- [ ] **500 g (1 lb) dried mixed fruit – choice fruits such as apricots, prunes, pears, apples or peaches**
- [ ] **1 tablespoon desiccated coconut**

MARINADE
- [ ] **1 L (1³/4 pts) strong cold tea**
- [ ] **1 tablespoon clear honey**
- [ ] **1 teaspoon lemon juice**

1   To make marinade, combine tea, honey and lemon juice. If necessary warm mixture slightly to dissolve the honey. Add fruit and set aside for 1-2 hours.
2   Thread fruit onto six wooden skewers and roll in coconut to lightly coat kebabs.

630 kilojoules (145 Calories) per serve

Fat	negligible	
Cholesterol	none	
Fibre	15.7 g	high
Sodium	30 mg	low

CUCUMBER BITES

These cool cucumber bites are a lovely refreshing mouthful for a hot summer's day. They can be made up, packed in lettuce leaves in their serving container and refrigerated until ready to go on the picnic. Dill sprigs make a pretty garnish.

Serves 6
- [ ] **1 large cucumber, cut into 2.5 cm (1 in) pieces**

FILLING
- [ ] **2 shallots, finely chopped**
- [ ] **¹/2 cup (125 g/4 oz) ricotta cheese**
- [ ] **¹/2 cup (125 g/4 oz) low-fat unflavoured yoghurt**
- [ ] **1 tablespoon finely chopped fresh mint**
- [ ] **1 tablespoon chopped fresh dill**
- [ ] **freshly ground black pepper**

1   Using a melon baller remove the centre from each cucumber piece, leaving enough to form a base. Discard the centres.
2   To make filling, place shallots, ricotta, yoghurt, mint and dill in a bowl and mix well to combine. Season to taste with pepper. Spoon filling into cucumber pieces and serve.

190 kilojoules (45 Calories) per serve

Fat	2.5 g	high
Cholesterol	11 mg	low
Fibre	0.2 g	low
Sodium	65 mg	low

VEGETABLE BUNDLES WITH GUACAMOLE

Serves 6
- [ ] **2 large carrots, cut into thin sticks**
- [ ] **500 g (1 lb) fresh asparagus, trimmed**
- [ ] **250 g (8 oz) fresh green beans, trimmed**
- [ ] **long chives, blanched**

GUACAMOLE
- [ ] **2 avocados, seeded, peeled and chopped**
- [ ] **¹/2 cup (125 g/4 oz) low-fat unflavoured yoghurt**
- [ ] **2 tablespoons lime juice**
- [ ] **Tabasco sauce**
- [ ] **freshly ground black pepper**

1   Boil, steam or microwave carrots, asparagus and beans separately until just tender crisp. Refresh under cold running water and set aside.
2   Trim carrots, asparagus and beans to about the same length. Divide vegetables into bundles and tie with chives. Refrigerate until ready to take on the picnic.
3   To make guacamole, place avocados, yoghurt and lime juice in food processor or blender and process until smooth. Season to taste with Tabasco sauce and pepper. Transfer to a small covered bowl and refrigerate.

790 kilojoules (190 Calories) per serve

Fat	15 g	high
Cholesterol	negligible	
Fibre	4.0 g	medium
Sodium	40 mg	low

COOL IT

▲   Having plenty of cold drinks, especially plain water, mineral water and fruit juice, is something everyone appreciates on a warm day.

▲   It is essential to keep all food cool until it is eaten or cooked.

Salad in a Loaf, Cucumber Bites, Vegetable Bundles with Guacamole, Dried Fruit Medley

Party Time for Tots and Teens

Everybody loves a party and planning for it can be as much fun as the occasion itself.
Having a theme is a good start, pirates, outer space, fairies or ballerinas are all popular. The menu, decorations and games can be planned around the theme and the guests can come dressed up for even more fun.
Have the party over a normal mealtime and serve savoury foods followed by sweet treats rather than everything at once. Foods that are small or in individual serves and can be eaten with fingers are easiest with younger children. Teenagers may prefer to have a more sophisticated 'sit-down dinner'.

❖

BIRTHDAY CAKE

25 slices

The candles used in this recipe are available from most cake decorating supply shops.

- ☐ 1³/₄ cups (200 g/6¹/₂ oz) self-raising flour
- ☐ ¹/₂ teaspoon bicarbonate of soda
- ☐ 5 tablespoons cocoa
- ☐ 1¹/₂ cups (375 g/12 oz) sugar
- ☐ ¹/₂ cup (125 g/4 oz) polyunsaturated margarine or butter, melted
- ☐ 1 cup (250 mL/8 fl.oz) milk
- ☐ 1 teaspoon vanilla
- ☐ 2 eggs
- ☐ ¹/₂ teaspoon cochineal
- ☐ 3 tablespoons raspberry jam
- ☐ 1 cup (90 g/3 oz) shredded coconut
- ☐ Teddy bear candles

CHOCOLATE ICING
- ☐ 60 g (2 oz) polyunsaturated margarine or butter, softened
- ☐ 3-4 tablespoons low-fat milk
- ☐ 3 cups (500 g/1 lb) icing sugar
- ☐ 2 tablespoons cocoa

1   Sift flour, bicarbonate of soda and cocoa into a large mixing bowl. Add sugar, margarine, milk and vanilla. Beat well to combine and stir in eggs and cochineal, then beat lightly until mixture is smooth.
2   Pour mixture into two lightly greased 20 cm (8 in) shallow round cake pans. Bake at 190°C (375°F) for 30-35 minutes or until cooked when tested. Allow to cool in pans for 5 minutes before turning onto a wire rack to cool.
3   To make chocolate icing, combine margarine and milk. Mix in icing sugar and cocoa. Beat for 5 minutes or until mixture is light and fluffy.
4   Spread one cake layer with jam. Top with remaining cake layer. Spread top and sides of cake with chocolate icing and sprinkle with shredded coconut. Arrange candles on top of cake.

1140 kilojoules (270 Calories) per slice

Fat	*10 g*	*medium*
Cholesterol	*20 mg*	*low*
Fibre	*2.3 g*	*medium*
Sodium	*180 mg*	*low*

FOOD IDEAS

▲   For very small children serve a normal meal in an amusing way. For example, a fish finger engine with mashed potato smoke and a cargo of peas and corn, or a hamburger pattie hippo in a green bean swamp.

▲   Make pinwheel sandwiches by having a loaf of bread sliced lengthways. Use peanut butter, salmon paste, cottage cheese with chopped parsley, mashed egg or finely chopped chicken moistened with mayonnaise for fillings, roll up and cut into thin rounds.

▲   Have a party in the park. Pack an individual picnic for each child in brightly coloured lunch boxes.

TEDDY BEAR'S PICNIC

Spread a rug indoors or take a hamper to the park. Guests and their favourite teddies are invited.

△ Peanut butter and honey sandwiches

△ Tiny bacon and egg tarts

△ Cherry tomatoes, cheese sticks and celery sticks

△ Smartie cakes

△ Tiny porcupines

△ Honey malted milkshakes

❖

TINY BACON AND EGG TARTS

Makes 12 tartlets

☐ **3 sheets prepared shortcrust pastry, thawed**

FILLING

☐ **2 rashers lean bacon, rind removed**

☐ **2 eggs**

☐ **1 teaspoon plain flour**

☐ **1 cup (250 mL/8 fl.oz) milk**

☐ **3 slices cheddar cheese, cut into 1 cm ($^1/_2$ in) pieces**

1   To make filling, grill or microwave bacon until crisp, then cut 2 cm ($^3/_4$ in) pieces.

2   Combine eggs, flour and milk and set aside.

3   Cut pastry into rounds using a fluted pastry cutter and press into a lightly greased muffin pan.

4   Place a piece of cheese and bacon in each pastry case. Add a spoonful of egg mixture, making sure the tart is only about two-thirds full. Bake at 190°C (375°F) for 15-20 minutes or until golden and puffed.

790 kilojoules (190 Calories) per serve

Fat	*13 g*	*high*
Cholesterol	*55 mg*	*medium*
Fibre	*0.6 g*	*low*
Sodium	*235 mg*	*medium*

Birthday Cake, Tiny Bacon and Egg Tarts, Tiny Porcupines (page 90), Smartie Cakes (page 90)

TEEN'S PARTY

A PARTY FOR TEN

Dad can be guest chef at the barbecue, or if it looks like rain everything can be cooked ahead of time in the oven. Turn down the lights for the grand entrance of a spectacular birthday cake which doubles as dessert.

△ Kebabs
△ Chicken drumsticks
△ Fried rice
△ Coleslaw salad
△ Mixed bean salad
△ Rosemary bread
△ Brownies
△ Fruit punch

TINY PORCUPINES

Makes 50

- ☐ **250 g (8 oz) polyunsaturated margarine or butter**
- ☐ **1 cup (250 g/8 oz) sugar**
- ☐ **2 eggs**
- ☐ **3 cups (375 g/12 oz) self-raising flour, sifted**
- ☐ **1 cup (175 g/5^1/2 oz) sultanas**
- ☐ **1 teaspoon vanilla essence**
- ☐ **1 cup (45 g/1^1/2 oz) corn flakes**

1 Place butter and sugar in a large mixing bowl and beat until pale and creamy. Add eggs one at a time beating well after each addition until light and fluffy.

2 Fold in flour, sultanas and vanilla. Form into small balls and roll in corn flakes. Place on lightly greased oven trays and bake at 180°C (350°F) for 10-15 minutes. Transfer to wire racks to cool.

410 kilojoules (95 Calories) per biscuit

Fat	4.5 g	high
Cholesterol	9 mg	low
Fibre	0.4 g	low
Sodium	115 mg	low

VARIATION

For a really furry effect, roll the balls in unprocessed bran rather than corn flakes and bake as directed.

SMARTIE CAKES

Makes 12 cakes

- ☐ **60 g (2 oz) polyunsaturated margarine or butter**
- ☐ **^{1}/4 cup (60 g/2 oz) caster sugar**
- ☐ **^{1}/2 teaspoon vanilla**
- ☐ **1 egg**
- ☐ **1 cup (125 g/4 oz) self raising flour, sifted**
- ☐ **5 tablespoons milk**

GLACE ICING
- ☐ **1 cup (175 g/5^1/2 oz) sifted icing sugar**
- ☐ **1 tablespoon orange juice**
- ☐ **boiling water**
- ☐ **food colouring**
- ☐ **Smarties**

1 Cream butter and sugar until light and creamy. Add vanilla and egg, beat well until light and fluffy.

2 Fold in flour alternately with milk then spoon into small patty cases and bake at 190°C (375°F) for 15 minutes.

3 To make icing, place icing sugar in a mixing bowl. Add orange juice and a few drops of boiling water until icing reaches a spreading consistency. Colour as desired.

4 When the cakes are cold, ice and top with a Smartie.

710 kilojoules (170 Calories) per cake

Fat	5.5 g	medium
Cholesterol	20 mg	low
Fibre	0.3 g	low
Sodium	145 mg	low

ROSEMARY BREAD

You might like to make this bread using other fresh herbs such as thyme, parsley or dill.

20 slices

- ☐ **1 sachet (7 g/^{1}/4 oz) dried yeast**
- ☐ **1 teaspoon sugar**
- ☐ **1^1/4 cups (315 mL/10 fl. oz) warm water**
- ☐ **1^1/2 cups (200 g/6^1/2 oz) plain wholemeal flour**
- ☐ **1^1/2 cups (200 g/6^1/2 oz) plain flour**
- ☐ **2 tablespoons chopped fresh rosemary**
- ☐ **1 tablespoon vegetable oil**

1 Stir yeast and sugar into ^{1}/2 cup (125 mL/4 fl. oz) warm water and leave 15-20 minutes until frothy.

2 Sift wholemeal and plain flours into a large mixing bowl. Stir in rosemary. Make a well in the centre and pour in yeast mixture, oil and remaining warm water, stir until the dough forms a soft ball, cover with plastic food wrap and stand in a warm place for 30 minutes or until the dough has doubled in bulk.

3 Punch down and knead dough on a lightly floured surface for 5-10 minutes, using as little extra flour as possible.

4 Shape into a ball or into small individual balls for bread rolls. Dust with a little flour, cover with a clean cloth and leave for 30 minutes. Bake at 190°C (375°F) for 40 minutes for bread or 25 minutes for rolls.

320 kilojoules (75 Calories) per slice

Fat	1.5 g	low
Cholesterol	none	
Fibre	1.4 g	low
Sodium	negligible	

PARTY KEBABS

Kebabs are great party food as they are easy to eat standing up. Other vegetables such as zucchini or capsicum could also be used on the kebabs.

Serves 8

- ☐ **1 kg (2 lb) lean boneless lamb or beef, cut into 2.5 cm (1 in) cubes**
- ☐ **2 onions, cut into wedges**
- ☐ **20 cherry tomatoes**
- ☐ **20 button mushrooms**
- ☐ **fresh or drained canned pineapple, cut into chunks**

MARINADE
- ☐ **2 tablespoons polyunsaturated oil**
- ☐ **2 tablespoons vinegar**
- ☐ **1 clove garlic, crushed**
- ☐ **ground black pepper**

1 To make marinade, place oil, vinegar, crushed garlic and black pepper in a bowl, mix well to combine. Add meat and toss to coat with marinade. Refrigerate for 1-2 hours or overnight.

2 Thread meat onto lightly oiled wooden skewers alternately with onion, tomatoes, mushrooms and pineapple.

5 Grill or barbecue kebabs for 5-6 minutes, turning and basting with marinade frequently during cooking.

820 kilojoules (200 Calories) per serve

Fat	7 g	medium
Cholesterol	82 mg	medium
Fibre	1.9 g	low
Sodium	105 mg	low

*Chocolate Brownies (page 92),
Rosemary Bread; Mixed Bean Salad,
Bombe Vesuvius Birthday Cake (page 92);
Party Kebabs*

MIXED BEAN SALAD

Our bean salad is also great for picnics and vegetarian meals.

Serves 10

- ☐ **125 g (4 oz) fresh green beans, cut into 5 cm (2 in) lengths**
- ☐ **425 g (14 oz) canned four bean mix, drained and rinsed**
- ☐ **1 tablespoon olive oil**
- ☐ **2 tablespoons white vinegar**

1   Boil, steam or microwave green beans until just tender. Refresh under cold running water and drain.

2   Place bean mix and green beans in a salad bowl. Combine oil and vinegar and toss through beans. Refrigerate until ready to serve.

250 kilojoules (60 Calories) per serve

Fat	*2 g*	*medium*
Cholesterol	*none*	
Fibre	*4.1 g*	*medium*
Sodium	*140 mg*	*low*

CHOCOLATE BROWNIES

Real special occasion food, these brownies are sure to be popular.

Makes 20

- ☐ **³/₄ cup (90 g/3 oz) plain flour**
- ☐ **¹/₂ teaspoon baking powder**
- ☐ **¹/₂ cup (60 g/2 oz) cocoa**
- ☐ **1 cup (250 g/8 oz) sugar**
- ☐ **¹/₂ cup (125 g/4 oz) polyunsaturated margarine or butter, melted**
- ☐ **2 eggs, beaten**
- ☐ **1 teaspoon vanilla**
- ☐ **1 cup (125 g/4 oz) coarsely chopped nuts (walnuts, pecan, almonds)**

1   Sift flour, baking powder and cocoa into a large mixing bowl. Combine sugar, margarine and eggs, add to flour mixture and mix to combine. Stir in vanilla and chopped nuts.

2   Spoon mixture into a lightly greased 20 cm (8 in) square cake pan and bake at 190°C (375°F) for 30 minutes or until cooked when tested. Stand in pan for 5 minutes before turning onto a wire rack to cool. Cut into squares for serving.

670 kilojoules (160 Calories) per biscuit

Fat	*9.5 g*	*high*
Cholesterol	*22 mg*	*low*
Fibre	*1.7 g*	*low*
Sodium	*95 mg*	*low*

BOMBE VESUVIUS BIRTHDAY CAKE

Serves 15

- ☐ **2 litres (3¹/₂ pts) vanilla ice cream**
- ☐ **sponge cake or butter cake (may be stale)**
- ☐ **6 egg whites**
- ☐ **¹/₂ cup (125 g/4 oz) caster sugar**
- ☐ **1 egg shell**
- ☐ **Creme de Menthe (optional)**

1   Line 2 L (3¹/₂ pts) pudding basin with plastic food wrap. Spoon ice cream into pudding basin, packing down firmly, leaving 2.5 cm (1 in) at the top. Cut cake to fit the basin and place over ice cream making sure that the ice cream is completely covered by cake. Refreeze.

2   Just before serving, beat the egg whites until stiff peaks form. Add the sugar a little at a time, continue beating continually until sugar dissolves and mixture becomes thick and glossy.

3   Carefully unmould the ice cream and cake on to an ovenproof platter. Cover entire cake with beaten egg white mixture, making sure there are no holes.

4   Place in a hot oven – 220°C (425°F) – for 5-10 minutes until egg whites are just starting to colour slightly. Serve immediately.

5   For a spectacular effect, gently press half an eggshell into the top of the bombe. Fill with Creme de Menthe and set alight. Tilt gently from side to side so that flaming rivers of liqueur run down the sides.

800 kilojoules (190 Calories) per serve

Fat	*7 g*	*medium*
Cholesterol	*35 mg*	*low*
Fibre	*negligible*	
Sodium	*120 mg*	*low*

FOOD IDEAS

▲   Make a simple fruit punch using fruit juice and soda or mineral water.

▲   Make ice blocks from frozen fruit juice to add to the punch so it does not become watery when they melt.

▲   For nibbles make 'Nuts and Bolts'. Use unsalted nuts mixed with Nutri-Grain cereal.

▲   Have a platter of raw vegetables cut into straws and a bowl of garlic-flavoured mayonnaise for a dip.

PARTY POINTERS

▲   Casual help from family members or a neighbour's teenage child, or professional help from party organisers, can make a big difference if fifteen four-year-olds are arriving at 11 am next Saturday. Think about it!

▲   What's your action plan if the weather is against you? Will the party be postponed or moved to another venue? What's your cut-off time before Plan B goes into effect? Have you made alternative plans clear and put a contact phone number on the invitation?

▲   The small birthday boy or birthday girl should be told that the deal is as follows: you get all the presents because it's your party, but you are not supposed to win any of the games! The little prizes are for the guests. This advance warning could save an at-party tantrum.

▲   A simple rule of thumb with parents is to ask them to stay if the party is for under five-year-olds and to pray they'll leave if everyone is over five. If parents are staying, you could ask them to help but it's more likely that you'll end up entertaining them as well with morning or afternoon tea (or something stronger). So be prepared.

▲   Nine times out of ten, cocktail frankfurts will burst. Sausage rolls will be left in the oven too long and will burn. Your rock cakes will turn out to be aptly named. So have some spare supplies. While many parents contend that children don't eat at birthday parties, and say food is a marginal issue, any adults present will be looking forward to taking a stroll down a culinary memory lane. Even if the children couldn't care less, the adults will be expecting the treats fondly remembered from their youth.

▲   Getting slow-moving guests to go home so that you can put your feet up and survey the mess, can be a problem. So just whisper in any lagging child's ear that there are some great lolly bags and little treats for each child, but these are only being distributed to those children who are going. Child will make a beeline for the front door, dragging potential stop-out parents as well.

Balancing the Budget

Spend your food money wisely. Plan your menu, make a list and make it healthy too!

HIGH-FAT FOOD

Although polyunsaturated margarine and reduced-fat spreads and polyunsaturated oils, olive oil and canola oil are high-fat foods they also contain polyunsaturated and mono-unsaturated fats which are needed in the diet in small quantities.

Planning ahead helps to make the best use of the food money. Spending a little time with the family once a week, and planning your meals for the next week, will make it easier to avoid the last-minute use of prepared foods, which are usually more expensive.

Write out the week's menu, include some family favourites and keep variety in mind. It may help to work from our 'Suggested meal plan'.

Display the menu in the kitchen and involve all family members in food preparation. Children enjoy preparing meals; they will need some help at first, but will gradually become more expert.

Once the menu has been planned, check the foods needed and prepare a shopping list.

YOUR FOOD PURSE

Spend most of your food money on foods with a good balance of nutrients and kilojoules (calories). Fatty snack foods like potato crisps, sweet biscuits and pastries, soft drinks and cordials sweetened with sugar, lollies and chocolates are all examples of foods which supply kilojoules but few of the important nutrients. These are the foods where cuts can be made to save dollars.

Shopping

△ Prepare a shopping list and keep to it and avoid impulse buying
△ Avoid buying more than you need
△ If it is cheaper to buy large quantities, arrange to share the food and costs with friends and neighbours
△ Use house brands and generic items if they are of similar quality and cheaper than branded items
△ Buy fruits and vegetables in season
△ Compare the price of fresh, frozen and canned fruits, fruit juice and vegetables and make the best buy

At Home

△ Plan meals in advance
△ Avoid waste
△ Serve larger portions of potatoes, rice and pasta with smaller portions of meat, chicken and fish
△ Serve bread with meals
△ Use canned or dried peas, beans and lentils to replace some of the meat in casseroles, stews, savoury mince, soups, meatloaves and rissoles
△ Add oats, rice, bulghur (cracked wheat) or home-made breadcrumbs to mixtures for rissoles, meatloaves or stuffing
△ Use skim milk powder to replace fresh milk in cooking
△ Use low-fat yoghurt and ricotta cheese to replace cream
△ Prepare some 'fast food' at home - hamburgers and pizza
△ Keep cooking time to a minimum
△. Plan the use of the oven to cook more than one food at a time

WISE SHOPPING

A wise shopper keeps the Healthy Diet Pyramid in mind and checks labels carefully to avoid buying unnecessary fat, sugar and salt.

Depending on the menu for the week and the stores in the cupboard and refrigerator, the basic shopping list might include:

At the Supermarket
BUY MOST
△ Bread of all varieties, rolls, muffins and crumpets, including wholemeal and mixed grain varieties
△ Breakfast cereals – rolled oats, ready-to-eat cereals. Choose those with more dietary fibre and less fat, sugar and salt
△ Rice, preferably brown, pastas like spaghetti, macaroni and noodles, cracked wheat (bulghur), corn kernels (for 'popping'), wholemeal crispbreads
△ Canned fruit, canned vegetables, baked beans, canned kidney beans and bean mixes, dried peas, beans and lentils, canned tomato paste, frozen vegetables, dried fruit, fruit juice (canned, bottled or UHT)
BUY MODERATELY
△ Milk, including low-fat and reduced-fat , fresh, UHT, canned, or powdered
△ Cheese, including cottage and ricotta, and other reduced-fat and low-fat varieties
△ Custard – chilled or UHT
△ Eggs, canned fish (sardines, tuna, pink salmon), peanut butter, unsalted nuts
△ Fresh or frozen meat, chicken and fish
BUY IN SMALL AMOUNTS
△ Polyunsaturated margarine and reduced-fat spread, butter
△ Polyunsaturated oil, olive or canola oil
△ Sugar, honey and jam
△ Plain mineral water, soda water, soft drinks, cordials, confectionery

Extras
Tea, coffee, cocoa, dried herbs and spices

At the Fruit and Vegetable Market
Fresh fruits and vegetables in season. If possible buy these every two or three days

At the Butcher's/Chicken/Fish Shop
Lean meats, chicken and fish. Check for specials and recipe handouts Remember that 'good buys' available now can be frozen for later use.

Suggested Meal Plan

Breakfast

Fruit – fresh, canned, stewed or dried, or juice

Cereal – choose wholegrain

Milk/yoghurt – use some reduced-fat and low-fat

Toast/muffins/crumpets – choose some wholegrain

Polyunsaturated margarine/reduced-fat spread/butter – scraping only

Marmalade/jam/honey – optional

Lunch

Bread/bagels/pita/flatbread and/or pasta or rice – preferably wholemeal or mixed grain

Vegetables (including potato) – salad or cooked – fresh, canned, frozen or dried, or vegetable soup

Protein-rich food – small to medium serve of either lean meat, chicken, fish, eggs, 'yolk-free' egg mix, baked beans, cooked or canned dried peas, beans or lentils, bean curd (tofu), hummus, cheese, peanut butter

Fruit – fresh, canned, stewed or dried

Milk/yoghurt/ice cream and the like – milk, plain or flavoured, yoghurt, plain or fruit, custard, ice cream, milk ice confection. Use some low-fat and reduced-fat

Polyunsaturated margarine/reduced-fat spread/butter – scraping

Dinner

Follow the same outline as for lunch and use the recipes and suggestions throughout the book. Don't forget the potato. If you prefer, serve less bread, more potatoes and rice and pasta at dinner.

Snacks

For growing children and teenagers, and adults who are active and not overweight.

Takeaways

When you buy takeaway food, choose dishes with less fat, ask for no salt and combine the takeaway with some salad vegetables and fruit.

Glossary of Terms

TERM	MEANING
Bicarbonate of Soda	Baking Soda
Breadcrumbs, fresh	1 or 2 day old bread made into crumbs
Breadcrumbs, packaged	Use commercially packaged breadcrumbs
Butterfly pork steaks	Double pork loin steaks
Capsicum	Red or green bell peppers
Cheese, tasty	A firm good-tasting cheddar cheese
Chiko Roll	Meat and vegetables in a wonton wrapper and deep fried. Available from fast food outlets.
Copha	A solid fat made from coconut oil. A pure vegetable cooking fat can be used.
Cornflour	Cornstarch
Devon	Fritz or luncheon sausage
Eggplant	Aubergine
Evaporated skim milk	If unavailable use low fat evaporated milk
Ginger	Fresh ginger is ginger root. Preserved ginger is root ginger cooked in syrup
Green prawns	Uncooked prawns
Lebanese cucumber	Ridge cucumber
Light mayonnaise	A fat-reduced mayonnaise
Low-kilojoule fruit jam	No-added-sugar jam
Mignonette lettuce	A round lettuce with reddish leaves, sometimes called Four Seasons
Modified milks	Skimmed or semi-skimmed milks
Muffin pans	Deep tartlets pans, if unavailable line tartlet tins with paper cake cases
Patty pan	A sheet of tartlet tins
Polyunsaturated margarine	Use reduced-salt varieties
Polyunsaturated oil	A vegetable oil high in polyunsaturated fats such as corn, soya or sunflower
Ready-rolled puff or shortcrust pastry	Use just-thawed frozen puff or shortcrust pastry rolled out to required size
Rice bran	If unavailable substitute oat bran
Rockmelon	Galia melon
Seasoning	Stuffing
Shallots	Spring onions or scallions
Snow peas	Mangetout peas
Snow pea sprouts	Substitute any sprouted beans or seeds
Sour cream	Commercially soured cream
Four bean mix	Canned mixed beans
Three bean mix	Canned mixed beans
Tofu	Bean curd
Tomato paste	Tomato puree
Vegeroni noodles	A vegetable pasta
Weet-bix	Weetabix cereal
Yellow lentils	Yellow dhal available from Indian shops
Yolk-free egg mix	A low-cholesterol egg mix that can be used in place of whole eggs in cooking. If unavailable reconstituted dried egg white can sometimes be used.
Zucchini	Courgettes

Useful Information

In this book, ingredients such as fish and meat are given in grams and ounces so you know how much to buy. A small inexpensive set of kitchen scales is always handy and very easy to use. A nest of measuring cups (1 cup, $^1/_2$ cup, $^1/_3$ cup and $^1/_4$ cup), a set of spoons (1 tablespoon, 1 teaspoon, $^1/_2$ teaspoon and $^1/_4$ teaspoon) and a transparent graduated measuring jug (1 litre or 250 mL) for measuring liquids are all useful kitchen accessories and will make measuring ingredients accurate. All cup and spoon measures are level.

MEASURING UP

Metric Measuring Cups

$^1/_4$ cup	60 mL	2 fl.oz
$^1/_3$ cup	80 mL	$2^1/_2$ fl.oz
$^1/_2$ cup	125 mL	4 fl.oz
1 cup	250 mL	8 fl.oz

Metric Measuring Spoons

$^1/_4$ teaspoon	1.25 mL
$^1/_2$ teaspoon	2.5 mL
1 teaspoon	5 mL
1 tablespoon	20 mL

MEASURING LIQUIDS

Metric	Imperial	Cup
30 mL	1 fl.oz	
60 mL	2 fl.oz	$^1/_4$ cup
90 mL	3 fl.oz	
125 mL	4 fl.oz	$^1/_2$ cup
170 mL	$5^1/_2$ fl.oz	$^2/_3$ cup
185 mL	6 fl.oz	
220 mL	7 fl.oz	
250 mL	8 fl.oz	1 cup
500 mL	16 fl.oz	2 cups
600 mL	1 pint	

MEASURING DRY INGREDIENTS

Metric	Imperial
15 g	$^1/_2$ oz
30 g	1 oz
60 g	2 oz
90 g	3 oz
125 g	4 oz
155 g	5 oz
185 g	6 oz
220 g	7 oz
250 g	8 oz
280 g	9 oz
315 g	10 oz
350 g	11 oz
375 g	12 oz
410 g	13 oz
440 g	14 oz
470 g	15 oz
500 g	16 oz (1 lb)
750 g	1 lb 8 oz
1 kg	2 lb
1.5 kg	3 lb
2 kg	4 lb
2.5 kg	5 lb

QUICK CONVERTER

Metric	Imperial
5 mm	$^1/_4$ in
1 cm	$^1/_2$ in
2 cm	$^3/_4$ in
2.5 cm	1 in
5 cm	2 in
10 cm	4 in
15 cm	6 in
20 cm	8 in
23 cm	9 in
25 cm	10 in
30 cm	12 in

OVEN TEMPERATURES

°C	°F	Gas Mark
120	250	$^1/_2$
140	275	1
150	300	2
160	325	3
180	350	4
190	375	5
200	400	6
220	425	7
240	475	8
250	500	9

Index

ACKNOWLEDGEMENTS
The publishers wish to thank the following Admiral Appliances; Black & Decker (Australasia) Pty Ltd; Blanco Appliances; Green's General Foods Pty Ltd; Knebel Kitchens; Leigh Mardon Pty Ltd; Master Foods of Australia; Meadow Lea Foods; Namco Cookware; NSW Egg Corporation; Ricegrowers' Co-op Mills Ltd; Sunbeam Corporation Ltd; Tycraft Pty Ltd distributors of Braun, Australia; White Wings Foods for their assistance during recipe testing.

China Doll; Dasch; Flossoms; Hale Imports; Hampshire and Lounders; Isabella Fruit Palace; Lifestyle Imports; Made in Japan; Villa Italiana; Village Living for their assistance during photography.